SCOTTISH PRINTED BOOKS
1508–2008

Antony Kamm

Title page of Bellenden's translation into Scots of Boece's history of Scotland, printed by Thomas Davidson in about 1540.

ACKNOWLEDGMENTS

The author is especially indebted to the following members of the Rare Book Collections Division of the National Library of Scotland for their inspiration, practical editorial assistance, and unfailing patience and good humour: Robert Betteridge, Irene Danks, Anette Hagan, Brian Hillyard, Graham Hogg, Eoin Shalloo, and Helen Vincent. Particular thanks are due also to Patrick Mark, honorary chairman of the Scottish Printing Archival Trust, and Richard Honour for their advice on printing technology.

The hardback cover of *The Good Husband of Zebra Drive* on page 46 is reproduced by permission of Polygon, an imprint of Birlinn Ltd. Permission has also been granted by the copyright owners who are named in the captions to illustrations – SNPG stands for the Scottish National Portrait Gallery. Copyright in all unattributed images belongs to the National Library of Scotland.

The titles of books and the names of their authors follow those which are used in National Library of Scotland catalogues, to make it easier for readers of this book to identify them, and come and read the originals in the collections.

Every effort has been made to contact copyright holders. If any have been inadvertently missed, please contact the publishers.

The publishers are especially grateful to J. Thomson Colour Printers for their in-kind contribution to this book.

National Library of Scotland

SANDSTONEPRESS
CONTEMPORARY QUALITY READING

www.nls.uk

www.sandstonepress.com

Contents

James IV. *(SNPG)*

John Napier's logarithms, 1614.

Margaret Oliphant.

Foreword

Are the days of the book at an end? Some say yes, and point to an electronic future in which books will be a thing of the past and we shall all read on screen. Others say no, and draw attention to the fact that the physical thing we call the book is not only as much appreciated as it ever was, but also is being produced in increasing numbers. On balance, it would seem that the obituarists should put their pens away for the foreseeable future, and that the story so attractively told in Antony Kamm's guide still has chapters to come.

One part of the story of the book is set here in Scotland. As Antony Kamm demonstrates, Scotland has always punched above its weight when it comes to printing and publishing. Today the printing industry is certainly a shadow of its former self, but Scottish publishing has a long and vigorous history which is still being played out. The credit for this must be shared – by publishers, librarians, booksellers – indeed by all who have worked for the cause of books in Scotland. Scottish publishers, in particular, showed remarkable determination in the second half of the 20th century and into the first years of the current century. They refused to allow the great tradition of the Scottish-produced book to end in capitulation to centralising pressures and to economies of scale. And the result of this refusal is visible today in the large number of Scottish publishers who continue to bring out a broad range of titles. The story set out in this guide is the background to that, and it is a fascinating one which Antony Kamm tells with mastery and economy. There is much for Scotland to be proud of in these last five hundred years. And there will be more to come.

Alexander McCall Smith

1. Before Printed Books

The first books in Scotland were probably scrolls introduced by the Roman military who briefly occupied the region south of the Antonine Wall in the middle of the 2nd century AD. Roman reading matter of the time included historical and biographical works, and poetry and drama, in Greek as well as Latin, all laboriously copied out by slaves. Gradually, the scroll was replaced by the codex (plural, codices), originally a set of writing tablets or leaves of papyrus or wood, hinged together like the pages of a book.

Later, priests, monks, and educated scribes kept religious and secular literature alive by copying manuscripts and embellishing them. Codices were now made of sheets usually of vellum, folded and bound together in volumes. Possibly the oldest surviving manuscript book produced in Scotland is the pocket-size Book of Deer, a 10th-century gospel book which was in the possession of the Columban monastery of Old Deer in Aberdeenshire in the 11th century.

Above right: The tradition of decorating books involved a considerable amount of time and effort. The Iona Psalter was written and illuminated in Oxford between about 1180 and 1220, it is believed for Beatrix, first prioress of Iona.

Below: The Murthly Hours, a prayer book for lay people, was created in Paris in the 1280s, and has been in Scotland since at least 1421, when it belonged to the Lord of Lorne. (Left) Miniature of the Journey of the Magi by one of three English artists who, between them, illustrated the 23 devotional scenes at the beginning of the book. (Right) Within the decorated initial, which opens the section of Gradual Psalms, is an image of the owner reading her book of hours, while Jesus looks down on her. At the bottom of the page, a youth shoots at two flying birds.

Towards the end of the 14th century, Andrew Wyntoun, prior of St Serf's Inch, wrote in rhyming couplets his *Orygynale Cronykil of Scotland*, of which the last four books deal with events in Scotland's recent past. In Book Seven, he quotes the lament on the state of the country after the death of Alexander III which begins, 'Quhen Alexander our kynge was dede, / That Scotland lede in lauche and le (in law and order)', and is regarded as the oldest surviving example of Scottish verse.

Between 1512 and 1542, James MacGregor, dean of Lismore, assembled in Fortingall a select group of poets and scribes who compiled the most significant surviving collection of early Gaelic formal, occasional, and heroic verse. *The Book of the Dean of Lismore*, which contains 2,500 items, came to light in the 18th century.

John Barbour (c. 1320–95), archdeacon of Aberdeen, the earliest known Scottish poet, may have spoken to veterans of Bannockburn (1314). He describes the battle in the *Bruce*, his patriotic panegyric, in 13,550 lines of rhyming couplets, of Robert I's successful fight to free Scotland from English domination.

During the 15th century, literacy spread beyond the Church and the nobility to the Scottish lairds. The poet known as Blind Harry or Henry the Minstrel (c. 1440–92) catered to the market so successfully with his *Wallace* that between the first printed version in about 1508 and the Act of Union in 1707 it went through 23 editions. In 12,000 lines of heroic couplets, Sir William Wallace, guardian of Scotland and sworn enemy of the English, is presented as a lusty fighter and ladies' man.

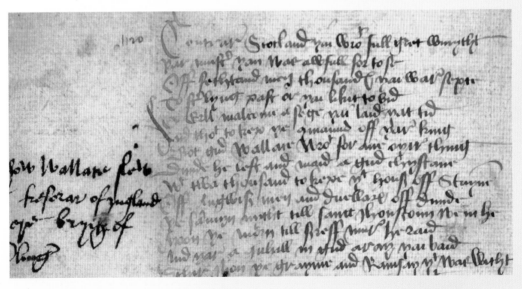

Above: Lines 1120-33 in the only surviving contemporary manuscript of the *Wallace*, written in 1488 by Prior John Ramsay of Perth. The note in the margin reads, 'How Wallace slew [the] tresorar (treasurer) of Ingland [at] the bryig (bridge) of [Ste]rling'. In 1995 an adaptation of the poem at several removes became the film *Braveheart*.

However late Scotland may have been among European nations in acquiring the craft of printing, the roots of the Scottish literary tradition had already been implanted at a time when Scots were writing and copying manuscript books of many kinds, and importing them from the Continent.

2. The First Printed Books

Printing from wooden blocks is considered to date back to the 8th or 9th century AD in China, and from wooden or ceramic movable type to the 11th century. Modern book printing, however, began in Europe in 1453–55 with a remarkable innovation. Johann Gutenberg, in his native town of Mainz, printed his Bible from movable metal type. Early printed books, however, maintained the manuscript tradition in that the type was designed to resemble handwriting and spaces were left for decorated initials or other illuminations to be inserted by hand. Wood block illustrations provided further decoration.

The printing press, like the European Renaissance itself, was slow to reach England, and even slower to come to Scotland. When William Caxton decided that it was time to transfer his press from Bruges to London in 1476, there were 70 towns on the Continent with printers. These were producing and distributing Latin and Greek classics, and theological and humanist works which were, in the enlightened reign of James IV, imported into Scotland or brought by returning or visiting scholars. James, himself a scholar as well as a man of action, was a new kind of king who embraced the ideas with which the Continent was buzzing and enthusiastically encouraged the development of Scottish learning, literature, and technology.

In the 15th century, works by Scottish scholars studying in Paris were printed there. The first texts by a Scottish author to be printed in his lifetime were two philosophical works by the Aberdonian James Liddell.

Left: William Elphinstone, bishop of Aberdeen, shared James IV's enthusiasm for the spread of learning. He founded King's College (1495), appointed Hector Boece as its principal, and attracted to it leading European scholars. Boece's history of Scotland (1527), was written in Latin and printed in Paris. By order of James V, it was translated into Scots by John Bellenden and printed in Edinburgh in about 1540 by Thomas Davidson, successor to Chepman and Myllar as the royal printer (see title page). *(University of Aberdeen)*

James IV and Elphinstone together provided the impetus for printing to begin in Scotland. On 15 September 1507, a royal patent was granted to Androw Myllar and Walter Chepman to establish a printing house in Edinburgh, with whatever foreign equipment and skills they required, to produce and sell law books, acts of parliament, religious books, lives of saints, and 'all other books that shall be deemed necessary'. It seems that Elphinstone had already had some of the religious books prepared for printing, notably the Aberdeen Breviary (*Breviarium Aberdonense*), designed for the clergy, and containing church services and practices according to Scottish traditions, with lives of local saints; it was produced in two volumes in 1510.

Below: Myllar's colophon is a pun on his name.

Both the new printers were already known at court. Myllar was originally a bookseller who had supplied books to the king. He had also printed in Rouen two books for the English market in 1505 and 1506 respectively. Chepman, a merchant who provided the money and the commercial know-how, was a former member of the royal household. Of the books we think were printed in 1508, their first year of business, all were in the Scots vernacular (a rarity in itself for an emergent national printing trade in those times), all could be said to have had a popular appeal, and all were in a portable (15 cm high) format. They included a translation of *De regimine principum bonum consilium* (Book of good counsel to the king), political commentary wrapped up in seven-line rhyming stanzas, and works by two of Scotland's most significant poets, Robert Henryson (d. 1490) and William Dunbar (c. 1460–1520).

Henryson, represented by his reworking of the legend of Orpheus and Eurydice as a Christian allegory and by two lesser poems, was probably a schoolmaster.

Below: Title page of Henryson's tale of Orpheus and Eurydice, with the device of Chepman incorporating the tree of knowledge, a standard symbol for printers of the time. The title reads, 'Heire begynnis the traitie (treatise, poem) of Orpheus kyng and how he yeid (went) to hewyn & to hel to seik his quene'.

Right: Henryson's *The Morall Fabillis of Esope the Phrygia*[n], 14 tales in verse lightly based on Aesop but set in the contemporary social climate of Scotland, was first printed in 1570. This edition, printed in 1571 by Thomas Bassandyne in Edinburgh, is set in *civilité*, a French typeface corresponding to the British 'secretary' hand which only appears in England five years later.

Dunbar was a renegade Franciscan friar and court hanger-on, who wrote religious poems, satirical poems, love poems, rude poems, moral poems, and poems of admonition and petition to the king. If we know something about him, it is because he is often autobiographical as he complains about his pension, grouses about the weather and his health, and harps on about his benefice. The books printed by Chepman and Myllar in 1508 include his topical ballad *Lord Barnard Stewart* (of which this is the only source), the long love poem *The Goldyn Targe*, and *The Flyting of Dunbar and Kennedy*, the earliest surviving example in Scots of that mixture of primitive literary criticism and lampoon.

The earliest Chepman and Myllar production that can be precisely dated (4 April 1508, printed at the end of the book) describes itself as *The Mayng or Disport of Chaucer*: it is not Scottish nor is it by Chaucer. It has been identified as *The Complaynte of a Loveres Lyfe* by an English priest, John Lydgate (c. 1370–1449). Geoffrey Chaucer (c. 1340–1400) was the most famous author of the age: Lydgate, a prolific poet, was a follower, sometimes an imitator, of Chaucer.

The third, and the most scholarly, of the great Scottish medieval poets was Gavin Douglas (c. 1474–1522), bishop of Dunkeld. His *Eneados*, a translation into Scots rhyming couplets of the twelve books of Virgil's *Aeneid*, was first printed in London in 1553 by William Copland.

3. Early Printing Methods

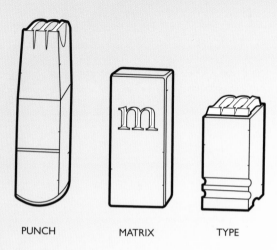

PUNCH   MATRIX   TYPE

The individual pieces of type were cast from a design engraved in relief onto a punch of hard metal, usually steel, which was driven into a block of copper to make the matrix. The part of the matrix carrying the character was held firm in a mould, into which was poured a molten blend of tin, antimony, and lead.

Two cases (an upper case for capitals and lower case for small letters) held the finished type, each character having a compartment of its own. A line at a time was assembled in a composing stick, and spaces inserted between the words to justify the line to the required length. After printing, the type was taken apart, cleaned, and distributed into its compartments in the cases.

The earliest printing machine was like a wine-or cheese-press. A vertical wooden screw raised and lowered the platen, the flat plate which pressed the paper onto the bed of type. On such a press, which was used by Gutenberg, 300 impressions could be made in a day.

In early modern Scotland there were effectively two kinds of book merchant: the printer, who may also have been a bookseller, and the bookseller, who may also have been a bookbinder. The burgh councils of Edinburgh, Aberdeen, and Glasgow controlled the admission to craft burgess or merchant guild membership. Apprentices joined the trade mainly for five or seven years, probably from the age of 17. Because of the restrictions on entry, the involvement of women was mainly informal: they helped in the family business, and sometimes inherited it.

Left: **Device of Jodocus Badius Ascensius (1462–1535), Belgian-born humanist and printer.**

A new kind of press, developed in Germany and in use in Scotland in the early 1580s, enabled 200 impressions an hour to be made. The screw was now metal, and a sliding bed allowed the type tray to be run in and out. The type, with leads added between the lines to space them apart, was held firm with wedges and locked in a metal (or sometimes wooden) frame called a chase. A frisket held the paper in place on the tympan, which folded onto the type.

TYPICAL HAND PRESS OF THE 17TH AND 18TH CENTURIES

(A) Screw, enclosed in casing

(B) Handle or lever

(C) Bed, on which the type is laid

(D) Frisket

(E) Tympan

(F) Platen

(G) Rounce, controlling the movement of the bed

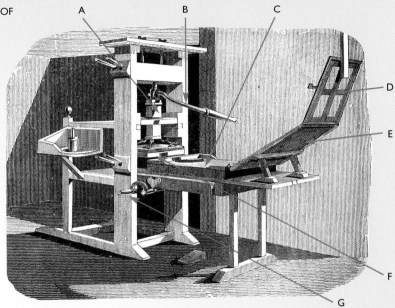

Printing a single sheet required nine separate operations. First, the dabbers or pelt balls (used in pairs) were covered with the sticky printer's ink, which was then applied to the surface of the type. A dampened sheet of paper was placed on the tympan, and frisket, paper, and tympan were folded over onto the type. The bed was then run under the platen, which was forced down on the paper by tightening the screw. Finally, the platen was lifted, the bed was pulled back, the tympan and frisket raised, and the sheet pulled clear. When all the sheets had been printed on one side, the process was repeated on the other side with a new setting of type, while the paper was still damp.

Paper was being manufactured from rags in England in the 15th century, and in Scotland from 1590 – before that, Scottish books were printed on paper imported from the Continent. The white cotton rags were sorted, cleaned, boiled, beaten into a pulp, and mixed with water. The resulting liquid was forced through a fine sieve, leaving the fibres on its surface, which was jogged to allow them to interlock. The individual sheets were then pressed, hung up to dry, and treated to give them a surface.

Right: Section of three sheets of folio, gathered to make twelve pages.

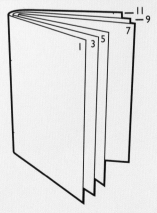

For binding, sheets taken from the press were folded once to make four pages (two leaves) folio size (fol. or 2°), twice for eight pages (four leaves) in quarto (4to or 4°), and three times for sixteen pages (eight leaves) in octavo (8vo or 8°). The sections were gathered, and then sewn together and into the casing (which might be of parchment, vellum, or leather), with the leaves trimmed or left uncut. Often the sections were simply stitched together with no cover, or were subsequently bound to the owner's taste.

In England, between 1586 and about 1640 printing was restricted by law to London, with one press each in the universities of Oxford and Cambridge, and was undertaken outside these places only clandestinely. In Scotland, during much the same period, new presses were set up in Stirling, Aberdeen, Glasgow, and (in 1651) Leith, joining those already established in Edinburgh and St Andrews.

4. Notable Early Books and their Printers

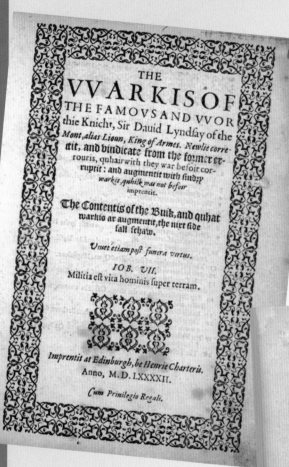

Left: The works of Sir David Lyndsay of the Mount (c. 1486–1555), keeper of the young king James V, Lyon King of Arms, poet, and dramatist. The book was first printed in 1568 by Henry Charteris (d. 1599), whose preface advocates printing Scottish literature in Scotland, and describes a performance in Edinburgh of Lyndsay's *Ane Pleasant Satyre of the Thrie Estaitis*, the first great Scottish drama, which lasted nine hours. Charteris was, as bookseller as well as printer, a major participant in the international book trade and, at a time when there were few presses, between 1586 and 1590 was the only printer in Scotland. The edition shown was printed in 1592.

Right: James VI, as poet, prose writer, and monarch, promoted printed works when other courts regarded them as vulgar. Authorship became respectable and the British book trade flourished. *Daemonologie*, printed in 1597 by Robert Waldegrave (c. 1554–1603/4), reflects the hysteria of the times and James's own preoccupation with witchcraft. Waldegrave, a Puritan sympathiser, left England, where he had printed subversive pamphlets, and was licensed to print in Edinburgh in 1590. Though he was appointed royal printer later that year, he produced works by Scottish Presbyterians, and in 1597 was tried for treason for printing without permission acts authorising Presbyterianism. He followed the king to London in 1603, but died shortly afterwards.

THeir beginnis the taill
of Rauf coilȝear how
he harbreit King
charlis

Imprentit at Sanc-
tandȝois be Robert Lekpreuik, Anno. 1572.

Above: Only one copy is known of the late-15th-century alliterative poem, by
an unknown Scot, of Rauf Coilyear (the Collier) and his wife, who entertain
Charlemagne unaware of who he is. It was printed in St Andrews in 1572 by
Robert Lekpreuik (fl. 1561–81), a supporter of the Reformed Church who
moved there from Edinburgh after being warned for printing uncensored
material. Back in Edinburgh in 1574, he was jailed for several years for
printing an anti-clerical poem. The title-page heads have nothing to do with
the story; they come from a book on physiognomy published in Strasbourg
in 1522.

Right: *A Choice Collection of Comic and Serious Scots Poems both Ancient and
Modern* was published in three volumes (1706, 1709, 1711) by James Watson
(c. 1664–1722), bookseller, and printer of over 500 titles, including the
newspapers the *Edinburgh Gazette* and *Edinburgh Courant*. The volumes
contributed to the revival of poetry written in Scots. A preface to *The
History of the Art of Printing*, published by Watson in 1713, outlines the
history of Scottish printing, without mentioning Chepman or Myllar or how
printing really began in Scotland.

A
Choice Collection
OF
COMIC and SERIOUS
Scots Poems
BOTH
ANCIENT and MODERN.

By several Hands. *James Watson*

PART I.

*Quicquid agunt Homines, votum, timor, ira, voluptas,
Gaudia, discursus, nostri est farrago Libelli.*

EDINBURGH,
Printed by *James Watson*: Sold by *John Vallange*.
M. DCC. VI.

5. Bibles and Prayer Books

The conflicts between Churches, and between Church authorities and the monarch, were largely responsible for the proliferation of catechisms, sermons, and exhortatory pamphlets and tracts which were printed in their thousands and distributed to people to read in their homes. Tracts could be produced comparatively cheaply; anyone with strong opinions, and the means, could promulgate their views. Eventually, as happened elsewhere, printing came to be associated with Protestantism and anti-Catholic material.

Right: **John Knox** *(SNPG: artist Adrian Vanson).*

John Knox (c. 1514–72), the architect of religious reform in Scotland, began his campaign in Geneva, where in 1558 he published *The First Blast of the Trumpet against the Monstruous Regiment* (rule) *of Women*. It was aimed at the Catholic rulers Mary Tudor in England and in Scotland Mary of Guise, regent for her teenage daughter, Mary, the Scottish queen but married to the dauphin of France. Knox was influenced by John Calvin (1509–64), organiser in Geneva of the Reformed faith. Calvin's theology was inspirational in the development of Protestantism and his ideas on Church government are the basis of Presbyterianism. Knox returned to Scotland in 1559 as minister of the High Kirk in Edinburgh, in which capacity he harassed Mary, Queen of Scots, from her arrival in Scotland in 1561.

Right: In March 1575 the General Assembly granted Thomas Bassandyne, a printer with Episcopalian leanings, and his partner Alexander Arbuthnet, a merchant, a licence to print Scotland's first indigenous Bible, a reprint of the second edition (1562) of the Geneva Bible in English. Because of delays, Bassandyne was forced in 1577 to hand over to Arbuthnet his completed sheets of the New Testament. He died the same year, and the Bassandyne Bible was published in 1579; Arbuthnet was now appointed royal printer. The page illustrated is from Exodus 14. The book is set throughout in roman type, in the same way as the other editions of the Geneva Bible, rather than the black letter type then in common use.

Robert Wedderburn (c. 1510–57) took holy orders as a priest, embraced Protestant doctrines, and became vicar of Dundee – his two sons were legitimised by royal favour. With his two older brothers he compiled, rewrote, or translated from German a lively collection of 'Godlie Psalmes and Spirituall Psalmes and Spirituall Sangis' celebrating the Protestant Reformation, first published anonymously in 1567, after all three were dead. The book was so popular that it was read to bits – only five copies survive from the editions printed in 1567, 1578, 1600, and 1621.

Right: The devotional *Ane Godlie Dreame*, 'written in Scottish metre' by Elizabeth Melville Colville and published by Robert Charteris (son and heir of Henry) in 1603, is the first book written by a woman to have been printed in Scotland.

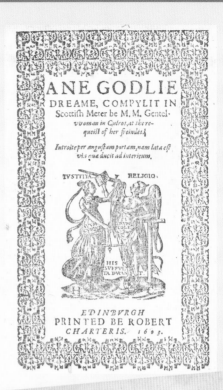

ANE GODLIE
DREAME, COMPYLIT IN
Scottish Meter be M. M. Gentel-
vuoman in Culros, at the re-
quest of her freindes.

Introite per angustam portam, nam lata est
via qua ducit ad interitum.

EDINBVRGH
PRINTED BE ROBERT
CHARTERIS. 1603.

Andro Hart (c. 1566–1621), though he was never royal printer, became closely associated with the Church of Scotland. The text of his edition of the Geneva Bible (1610), the second Bible to be produced in Scotland, was so accurate that it became standard for editions produced abroad. His widow continued the business after his death, under the imprint of 'Heirs of Andro Hart'. The Bassandyne and Hart Bibles were folio size, for the pulpit. The first two Scottish Bibles in a manageable octavo format were both printed in 1633 by Robert Young, who in 1638 produced a handier volume for a large-size pocket. Young, an Englishman who was appointed Scottish royal printer in 1632, left his English colleague Evan Tyler (d. 1682) to run his Edinburgh office. He shut down his Scottish business in 1638 and sold the equipment, but continued to act as royal printer from London. He was succeeded by Tyler in 1642.

Right: Charles I, in an attempt to continue the policy of his father, James VI, to promote Episcopacy in Scotland against the now entrenched Presbyterian opposition, invoked his royal prerogative to introduce a new service book in 1637. When readings from *The Booke of Common Prayer* (see right, open at the St Andrew's Day collect) were given in St Giles Cathedral in Edinburgh, there were riots, which led to the National Covenant being drawn up the following year. In 1640, the Scottish parliament abolished Church rule by bishops and freed itself from royal control. The subsequent military uprisings sparked off civil war, which ended with the execution of the king in 1649.

Saint Andrews day.

The Collect.

Almighty God, which didst give such grace unto thy holy Apostle Saint Andrew, that he readily obeyed the calling of thy Sonne Jesus Christ, and followed him without delay: grant unto us all, that wee being called by thy holy Word, may forthwith give over our selves obediently to fulfill thy holy Commandements, through the same Jesus Christ our Lord. Amen.

The Epistle.

Rom.10.9

If thou shalt confesse with thy mouth the Lord Jesus, and shalt beleeve in thine heart, that God hath raised him from the dead, thou shalt bee saved. For with the heart man beleeveth unto righteousnes, and with the mouth confession is made unto salvation. For the scripture saith, whosoever beleeveth on him, shall not be ashamed. For there is no difference betweene the Jew and the Greek: for the same Lord over all, is rich unto all that call upon him. For whosoever shall call upon the name of the Lord, shall be saved: How then shall they call on him in whom they have not beleeved? and how shall they beleeve in him of whom they have not heard? and how shall they heare without a preacher? And how shall they preach, except they be sent? as it is written, How beautifull are the feet of them that preach the gospel of peace, and bring glad tidings of good things? But they have n

Tyler's successor, Andrew Anderson (c. 1635–76), became royal printer in 1671, for the unprecedented term of 41 years, with patents and privileges which effectively put him in control of the Scottish printing trade. Yet, earlier that year, he had been ordered by the Privy Council of Scotland to withdraw an edition of the New Testament until its numerous errors had been corrected. He died considerably in debt and embroiled in court cases. His widow Agnes inherited the business, and the litigation, and thrived.

The first books printed in Gaelic were translations of religious works: Knox's book of Common Order (1567), Calvin's *Catechism* (1631), and the first 50 psalms (1659). The New Testament in Gaelic appeared in 1766, and the entire Bible finally in 1802.

Right: The New Testament in Irish Gaelic was published in Ireland in 1602, and the Old Testament in 1642. Their transliteration into roman characters (1690, see right) for readers in Scotland was undertaken by Robert Kirk (1644–92), minister of Aberfoyle, who had previously made the first translation into Scottish Gaelic of the complete Psalter (1684). Kirk justified his interest in the supernatural by setting out in scientific terms the results of his researches into the existence of another world in *The Secret Commonwealth of Elves, Fauns, and Fairies*, not published until 1893. He died, if he did die, while taking the air in his nightshirt on a fairy mound near his manse. It was believed that his spirit was removed and held captive by the fairies, who feared he might reveal the secrets of their ways of life.

AN
BIOBLA
NAOMHTHA,
IONA BHFUIL
Leabhair na Seintiomna
Ar na ttarruing as an EABHRA go Gaoidheilg
tré chúram agus dhúthrachd an Doctuir,
VILLIAM BEDEL,
Roimhe so, Easbug Chille móire a Néirinn:
AGUS
Na Tiomna Nuaidhe,
Ar na ttabhairt
Go fírinneach as GREIGIS go Gaoidheilg, re
VILLIAM O DOMHNVILL.

Left: Distinctive Scottish herringbone design on a Bible printed in 1715. It is so called because of the vertical stem in the centre panel of the cover, with pairs of tools set symmetrically on either side.

6. Politics, Proclamations, and the Secret Press

The earliest edition of parliamentary acts in book form was printed by Thomas Davidson, royal printer, in 1542. To be official printer to the king did not necessarily mean freedom from licensing restrictions, but it helped. Heresy and causing offence against the Crown, which were at various times punishable by death, provided a legal basis for censorship. A statute of 1552 gave the local bishop responsibility for licensing, and prescribed the penalties of confiscation and banishment for breaking the law. There ensued an uneasy situation, inflamed by the perceived danger of Catholic literature. In 1690, William and Mary's privy council made criticism of government the sole reason for legal action. In the meantime, some books had been banned, and six Scots had at various times been executed for contravening the law.

Below: *Forsamekill* (forasmuch) *as the contempt of the Kingis Maiesteis authoritie*, a royal proclamation on the enforcement of outlawing, printed in 1570 by Robert Lekpreuik, printer to the infant king, James VI. The body of the text and the imprint at the foot are in traditional black letter type, but the heading and tailpiece are in roman capitals. Thomas Davidson was the first printer in Scotland to import the roman typeface from the Continent. Lekpreuik, however, was the first to adopt it comprehensively.

APVD EDINBVRGH XXVII DIE MENSIS
DECEMBRIS. ANNO. DO. MILLESIMO QVINGENTESIMO
SEXAGESIMO NONO.

Forsamekill as the contempt of the kingis Maiesteis authoritie, of the Lawis and ordinar Justice of this Realme is the ground and fontane, fra quhilk all confusioun proceidis. And amangis vtheris euillis, the disobedience of the proces of horning, with the defoirsing of ordinar Officiaris in thair executiounis, is sa greit and

bring thame to the Lawis. And ordanis letteris to be direct for publicatioun heirof at all mercat Croces, and vtheris places neidfull as effeiris.

Imprentit at Edinburgh be Robert Lekpreuik
Printar to the kingis Maiestie. Anno. Do. 1570.

GOD SAVE THE KING

A TREATISE
CONCERNING
THE DEFENCE OF THE
HONOVR OF THE RIGHT
HIGH, MIGHTIE AND NOBLE PRINcesse, Marie Queene of Scotland, and Douager of France, with a Declaration, as wel of her Right, Title and Interest to the Succession of the Croune of England: as that the Regiment of Women is conformable to the lawe of God and Nature.

Made by Morgan Philippes, Bachelar of Diuinitie, An. 1570.

Left: John Leslie (1527–96), bishop of Ross and chief adviser to Mary, Queen of Scots, on religious affairs, was an indefatigable propagandist for her cause. This justification of her claim to the English Crown was printed in Liège in 1571 by John Fowler (1537–79), the most significant English printer/ publisher of the times. Though an edition (printed in Rheims) had appeared in London in 1569, the book would not have been allowed to be printed in post-Reformation Scotland.

Right: George Buchanan (1506–82), humanist and historian who wrote in Latin, was tutor to Mary, Queen of Scots, on her return to Scotland in 1561. This was in spite of his Protestant inclinations, which he openly declared by his support of the new General Assembly of the Church of Scotland. Relations with the queen went sour after the murder of her husband, Lord Darnley, and even sourer when in 1571, after she had been imprisoned in England, Buchanan published *De Maria Scotorum regina . . .*, a vicious attack on her in which he quoted from the notorious 'Casket Letters' – it was translated into Scots the same year. His *De jure regni apud Scotos* (1579), which justified her removal, was banned in Scotland more often than any other book between 1584 and 1688, and probably prevented Henry Charteris from being appointed royal printer to James VI. *(SNPG: artist Arnold Bronkorst)*

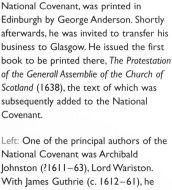

Left: *The Confession of Faith of the Kirk of Scotland* (1638), otherwise known as the National Covenant, was printed in Edinburgh by George Anderson. Shortly afterwards, he was invited to transfer his business to Glasgow. He issued the first book to be printed there, *The Protestation of the Generall Assemblie of the Church of Scotland* (1638), the text of which was subsequently added to the National Covenant.

Left: One of the principal authors of the National Covenant was Archibald Johnston (?1611–63), Lord Wariston. With James Guthrie (c. 1612–61), he wrote an explosive pamphlet, *Causes of the Lord[']s Wrath against Scotland*, printed by George Anderson's son Andrew in Edinburgh in 1653. It criticised Charles II, who had been crowned king of Scotland after signing the Covenant, and other backsliders and defectors from its precepts. For this, after the Restoration in 1660, Guthrie was hanged, and his head impaled in public view, where it remained for 28 years. Johnston, who had taken office under Cromwell, was executed in 1663.

(SNPG: artist George Jamesone)

Under the imprint of the 'Heir of Andrew Anderson', Agnes Anderson (1637–1716), widow of Andrew, inherited the post of royal printer and developed the business until it was the largest in Scotland, employing 16 apprentices. Though her standards of printing were notoriously lax, she was a sharp businesswoman and a frequent and generally successful litigant in protecting her interests. After campaigning for the office for two decades, she was finally appointed printer to the Church of Scotland in 1712. At her death, her estate was valued at £78,000 Scots, a vast sum in Scottish terms, equivalent to over £800,000 today.

Right: Agnes Anderson, as royal printer, issued this act of 1676 immediately after her husband's death. It prohibited the importation of Bibles from abroad in order to maintain his monopoly as the king's printer, in favour of his heir, who was herself.

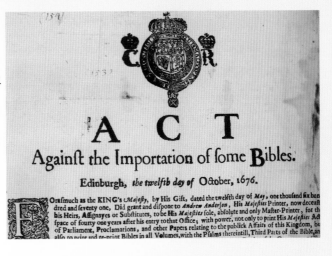

Right: George Mosman, printer to the Church of Scotland, surreptitiously printed A Wish for Peace in 1690, criticising the government. He was arrested and imprisoned. His excuse that the licensing system had not been much observed lately was dismissed, but he was subsequently released on payment of a bond against good behaviour in future.

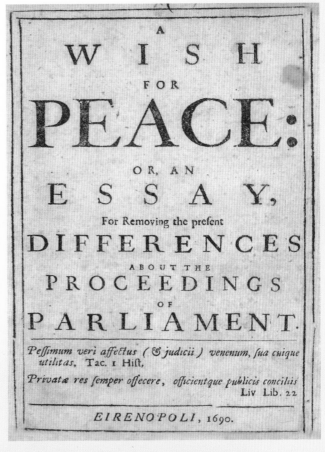

The National Covenant, the Civil War in the 1640s, the Act of Union, the Jacobite cause and rebellion of 1745, and its grim aftermath, were the subjects of bitter controversy in print.

Below: On 23 July 1745, with Charles Edward Stuart landed on Scottish soil to claim the crowns of England and Scotland on behalf of his father, the British government offered a reward of £30,000 for his arrest. The prince's proclamation in response, printed in Edinburgh, naming himself regent of Scotland, England, France, Ireland, and their dominions, offered the same sum for the arrest of the elector of Hanover, i.e. George II.

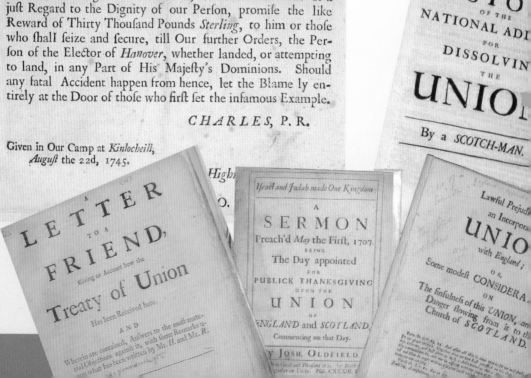

CHARLES
Prince of *Wales*, &c.

Regent of the Kingdoms of *Scotland*, *England*, *France* and *Ireland*, and the Dominions thereunto belonging.

HEREAS We have seen a certain scandalous and malicious Paper, published in the Stile and Form of a Proclamation, bearing Date the 1st instant, wherein under Pretence of bringing Us to Justice, like Our Royal Ancestor King *Charles* the I. of blessed Memory, there is a Reward, of Thirty Thousand Pounds *Sterling*, promised to those who shall deliver Us into the Hands of Our Enemies : We could not but be moved with a just Indignation at so insolent an Attempt. And tho' from Our Nature and Principles We abhor and detest a Practice so unusual among Christian Princes, We cannot but out of a just Regard to the Dignity of our Person, promise the like Reward of Thirty Thousand Pounds *Sterling*, to him or those who shall seize and secure, till Our further Orders, the Person of the Elector of *Hanover*, whether landed, or attempting to land, in any Part of His Majesty's Dominions. Should any fatal Accident happen from hence, let the Blame ly entirely at the Door of those who first set the infamous Example.

CHARLES, P. R.

Given in Our Camp at *Kinlocheill*, *August* the 22d, 1745.

Below: The union of the parliaments of Scotland and England generated as much controversy as its possible dissolution does today, but in more vitriolic language. Below, a selection of pamphlets of the time, some of them issued secretly.

THE
HISTO
OF THE
NATIONAL ADI
FOR
DISSOLVIN
THE
UNIO
By a *SCOTCH-MAN*.

A
LETTER
TO A
FRIEND,
Giving an Account how the
Treaty of Union
Has been Received here.
AND
Wherein are contained, Answers to the most mate-
rial Objections against it, with some Remarks u-
pon what has been written by Mr. H. and Mr. R.

Israel and Judah made One Kingdom
A
SERMON
Preach'd *May* the First, 1707.
BEING
The Day appointed
FOR
PUBLICK THANKSGIVING
UPON THE
UNION
OF
ENGLAND and SCOTLAND,
Commencing on that Day.
By JOSH. OLDFIELD

Lawful Prejudi
an Incorpora
UNIO
with *England* ;
OR
Some modest CONSIDERA
ON
The sinfulness of this UNION, an
Danger flowing from it to th
Church of SCOTLAND

7. Books for Learning

By 1500, Scotland had three universities (St Andrews, Glasgow, and King's College, Aberdeen), and a grammar school in each major town. Though Bishop Elphinstone's education act (1496) required those holding land from the Crown and freeholders of substance to put their eldest sons through grammar school and higher education, this was more an attempt to train potential lawyers than establish a universal education system. John Knox's First Book of Discipline, however, did contain the elements of a compulsory national scheme, for children who were 'apt for letters and learning'. It was written in 1560, probably by six ministers, including Knox, all called John, and was first published on the Continent in 1621 from an unknown manuscript. Though the plan itself failed to be ratified, the ideals behind it survived.

Right: The Catechisme (1552), a product of the Catholic Church, reflects the spread of printing by being the first book to be printed in St Andrews. Though aimed at the clergy rather than ordinary people, it was written in Scots as well as Latin. Here is the Lord's Prayer in Latin (above) and in Scots (below).

The new ministers of the Reformed Church were university trained; they taught children the catechism, and to read the Bible and prayers, and gave them lessons in Latin, which was the medium of instruction and conversation in grammar schools. By 1570, most towns had a grammar school. The burgh councils of Edinburgh and Glasgow established grammar-school curricula, regulated schools, stimulated the printing of schoolbooks, and, in the case of Edinburgh, financed in 1658 a grammar-school library. In other provincial towns, schoolmasters wrote books which were printed locally for use in their own classrooms. The burgh of Aberdeen, through a close relationship with the colleges there, published sermons and academic works, dedicated to the provost or other municipal dignitaries.

Right: This sheet for a hornbook was printed by Edward Raban in the 1620s. He was an Englishman who learned printing in Leiden. In 1620 he set up the first press in Aberdeen, to print books for King's and Marischal colleges, and for the town council.

Below: Hornbooks were so called because a sheet, printed with the alphabet, numbers, and sometimes prayers, and pasted onto a wooden board, was sometimes covered with a thin layer of cattle horn.

Whatever the upheavals between king and country, and between Churches, all were agreed on the need for education. Acts of parliament in 1633, 1646, and 1696 called for a school in every parish, even if school and schoolmaster were to be financed by local land holders. In 1755, there were, for instance, seven schools in the parish of Blair Atholl, with in all 250 pupils, many of them extremely poor. An answer to an enquiry by the Scottish Society for the Propagation of Christian Knowledge suggested that even if the society's funds would not allow it to pay schoolmasters who had no income other than from the parents, it might at least supply some books.

David Wedderburn, a schoolmaster, was in 1620 appointed poet laureate of Aberdeen. In 1632 he was given the freedom of Dundee for his textbook on Latin grammar. He also wrote *Vocabula* (1636), a Latin conversation book and word guide 'for beginners'. His definitions of *Arcus* (archery), *Pila Pedalis* (football), *Globi* (bowls), *Baculus* (golf), and other sports include (in Latin) terms familiar to modern fans.

Right: Peter Rae (1671–1748), minister in Kirkbride, set up in the manse in 1711 a press of his own construction. That year he printed *A New Method of Teaching the Latine Tongue* (104 pages) by John Hunter, and in 1712 *A Discourse against Swearing and Cursing* (12 pages) by William Assheton, rector of Beckenham, Kent, a reprint of a tract first published in 1692. The printer of both is named as his son Robert, probably to divert criticism from his congregation, for the boy was only eight at the time. If so, the subterfuge failed, as in 1713 Rae was censured for neglecting his pastoral duties for printing, and for issuing the 'obscene ballad of Maggie Lauder'. Rae, who was also a clockmaker, moved to Dumfries in 1715, where he persevered with his hobby, and published anonymously in 1718 a classic source of reference, *The History of the Late Rebellion* [of 1715], researched, written, and printed by himself. *(Gracefield Arts Centre, Dumfries)*

One of the leading educational publishers of the early 18th century was Thomas Ruddiman (1674–1757). He left home at 16 without his parents' knowledge to compete for the annual prize in classics at King's College, Aberdeen, which he won. In 1706 he began working for the Edinburgh printer and bookseller, Robert Freebairn, as proofreader and editor, while employed as a librarian in the Advocates' Library, of which he became keeper in 1730. With his brother Walter, he established a printing business in about 1715, principally to produce schoolbooks. Their best-known title was Ruddiman's own *Rudiments of the Latin Tongue*, first printed by Freebairn in 1714. In 1729 Ruddiman bought the mildly pro-Jacobite thrice-weekly *Caledonian Mercury* (founded 1720). It remained in his family until 1772, having become the most successful early Scottish newspaper.

The first book on book-keeping published in Scotland was *Idea Rationaria, or the Perfect Accomptant* (1683) by Robert Colinson, an Edinburgh teacher of accounting who had previously been a merchant in the Netherlands. For the next century, many of the most significant books on book-keeping were published in Scotland or were written by Scots. Among them was the standard accounting text of its time in Britain and north America, *Book-keeping Methodiz'd* (1736), by John Mair (1702/3–69), a master at Ayr Grammar School and later rector of Perth Academy. He was also a prolific writer of textbooks on Latin grammar.

William Smellie (1740–95) was given time off from his apprentice duties as corrector to a printing house to study arts and medicine at Edinburgh University. Subsequently he employed his medical knowledge in the printing and publishing trade to produce significant scientific works which, in turn, brought to his business leading authors of the times. He also made the *Edinburgh Magazine and Review*, which he owned 1773–76 and mainly wrote himself, one of the most talked about magazines in Britain.

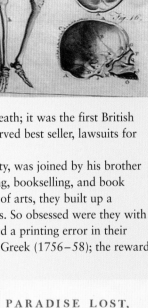

Encyclopaedia Britannica, published in Edinburgh from its launch in 1768 until 1901, is the oldest surviving English-language encyclopaedia, and was the first to group related topics into longer essays, which were then listed alphabetically. It was the idea of the Edinburgh master printer, Colin Macfarquhar (1744/5–1793), and the engraver Andrew Bell (1725/6–1809). As editor, they employed William Smellie. Much of the first edition of *Britannica*, published in 100 parts (1768–71), and in three volumes in 1771, was written by Smellie or copied by him from other publications. Some of Bell's engravings caused offence, and George III insisted that the plates of three of them, in the section on midwifery, should be ripped out of every copy.

Smellie was replaced as editor for the enlarged second edition (1778–83). Macfarquhar himself edited the third edition (1788–97) until his death; it was the first British encyclopaedia with multiple contributors, and though it was a deserved best seller, lawsuits for piracy were brought against its publisher.

In 1744, Robert Foulis (1707–76), printer to Glasgow University, was joined by his brother Andrew (1712–75). While involving themselves also in bookbinding, bookselling, and book distribution, and the establishment in the university of an academy of arts, they built up a reputation for the design and production of classical and other texts. So obsessed were they with perfection that they offered 1,000 guineas to anyone who discovered a printing error in their celebrated four-volume edition of the complete works of Homer in Greek (1756–58); the reward was never claimed.

PARADISE LOST,

A P O E M.

THE AUTHOR

JOHN MILTON.

GLASGOW:
PRINTED BY ROBERT AND ANDREW FOULIS,
PRINTERS TO THE UNIVERSITY,
M.DCC.LXX.

8. Science, Technology, and Medicine

The 16th, 17th, and 18th centuries were particularly fruitful for Scottish works on technology and other aspects of science, especially medicine. Robert Lekpreuik printed in Edinburgh in 1568 the first Scottish medical book, an account by Gilbert Skeyne (c. 1522–99), teacher of medicine at King's College, Aberdeen, of the plague that year in Edinburgh, with measures on treatment and the avoidance of infection. *Ane Breve Descriptioun of the Pest*, of which the only known copy is in the National Library of Scotland, was written in Scots, with the prescriptions in Latin. Skene subsequently became physician to James VI.

Below: To keep the type from which books were printed, in the event of a reprint, took up space, and was wasteful if type was in short supply, as it was in 1725 because of a lack of type founders in Scotland. To set it up again, and risk introducing errors, was laborious, especially if it was for a long book. William Ged (1684/5–1749), an Edinburgh goldsmith, responded to the challenge by making a mould of the type in plaster of Paris and, from this, casting a complete printing plate in metal, later known as a stereotype, or stereo. The process had been introduced in Holland a few years earlier, but Ged did not know this and was the first person in Britain to make and use a stereotype plate. The illustration shows part of the demonstration stereotype plate of eight pages, presented by Ged to the Faculty of Advocates in 1740.

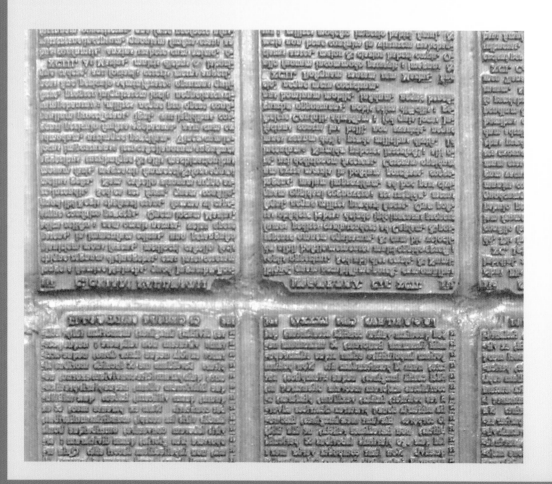

Domestic Medicine, or, The Family Physician (1769) by William Buchan (1729–1805) was the first popular medical book in English. It was edited and printed by William Smellie, but self-published by the author on 'subscription': that is, he solicited, and encouraged others to solicit on his behalf, orders before the book went to press. He asked Smellie to quote for an incredible print run of 10,000 copies, but in the end settled for 5,000, which were quickly sold in Scotland alone. Subsequent editions (17 in his lifetime, during which the book grew to 750 pages) were published in Edinburgh and London by a consortium of publishers, while Continental translations were produced in seven different languages.

Right: It is said that after the first edition Buchan sold the copyright of his book for £700, less than the publishing profit made each year from its sales. He ended his life in severe financial difficulties, having lost his wife's fortune.

Below: Alexander Monro (1733–1817) was the second and most distinguished of three generations of Monros who taught medicine at Edinburgh University. The illustrations are from *Observations on the Structure and Functions of the Nervous System* (1783), in which he describes his discovery of the communication between the lateral ventricles of the brain, now known as the foramen of Monro.

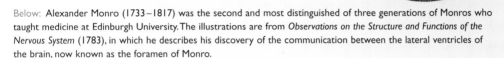

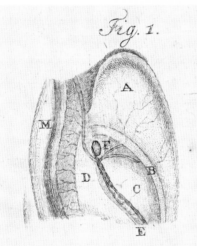

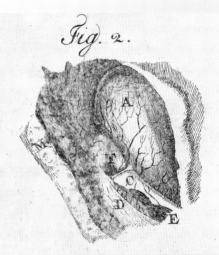

Right: John Napier advocated manuring land with common salt, and also patented a device for draining mines. He projected various war machines, including mirrors for burning enemy ships, a scatter-shell, and a tank propelled by infantry within which it would withstand the fire of a 'dooble musket'. *(Science and Society)*

In 1614, John Napier (1550–1617) of Merchiston, mathematician, inventor, and also theologian, published in Edinburgh his astonishing contribution to mathematical calculation. Written in Latin, the European language of scholarship of the times, it described his invention of logarithms, a method of simplifying complex calculations by addition or subtraction and the use of tables. Though logarithms were finally replaced in the 1970s by the electronic calculator, their benefit to mathematics can be compared with that of the invention of the computer. Three years later, the same printer, Andro Hart, produced *Rabdologiæ . . .*, in which Napier described a series of calculating devices, including the one known ever since as 'Napier's bones'.

Below: Another mathematician with a practical turn of mind was George Brown (1650–1730), a dissenting minister, who patented, and constructed, a 'Rotula arithmetica', which he claimed could do addition, subtraction, multiplication, and division. He also published a book on decimals (1701) and in 1718 a ready reckoner, which gave the decimal equivalents to seven places of amounts up to a pound, in farthing steps (see illustration).

2 M	Per An: At 1 £ per Cent	Per An: At 1¼ £ per Cent	Per An: At 1½ £ per Cent	Per An: At 1¾ per Cent
1	000.010000	000.012500	000.0150000	000.0175000
2	000.020000	000.025000	000.0300000	000.0350000
3	000.030000	000.037500	000.0450000	000.0525000
4	000.040000	000.050000	000.0600000	000.0700000
5	000.050000	000.062500	000.0750000	000.0875000
6	000.060000	000.075000	000.0900000	000.1050000
7	000.070000	000.087500	000.1050000	000.1225000
8	000.080000	000.100000	000.1200000	000.1400000
9	000.090000	000.112500	000.1350000	000.1575000

M	Per:Diem At 1 £ p:C:p: An	Per Diem At 1¼ £ p:C:p: An	Per:Diem At 1½ £ p:C:p: An	Per:Diem At 1¾ £ p:C:p: An
1	.000027397260	.000034246575	.000041095890	.000047945205
2	.000054794520	.000068493150	.000082191780	.000095890410
3	.000082191780	.000102739725	.000123287670	.000143835615
4	.000109589040	.000136986300	.000164383560	.000191780820
5	.000136986300	.000171232875	.000205479450	.000239726025
6	.000164383560	.000205479450	.000246575340	.000287671230
7	.000191780820	.000239726025	.000287671230	.000335616435
8	.000219178080	.000273972600	.000328767120	.000383561640
9	.000246575340	.000308219175	.000369863010	.000431506845
£1 M L		.001041666666	.001250000000	.001458333333

Gardeners in Scotland have not been well served with practical books: surprisingly, because the climate is diverse and the growing seasons are different from those in the south. What should have been a rich tradition began in 1683 with the publication of *The Scots Gard'ner* by John Reid (1656–1723), who practised gardening on various Scottish estates before emigrating to New Jersey, where he became surveyor-general of the province. His book is sometimes also regarded as the first Scottish cookery book, in that it includes an appendix on preserving and cooking fruits and vegetables. Also in 1683, Reid's friend John Sutherland (1638?–1719), first superintendent of the Physic Garden (later the Royal Botanic Garden) in Edinburgh, published a catalogue of its plants.

Below: Sir Robert Sibbald (1641–1722) trained as a doctor but was fascinated by geography and natural history, becoming geographer royal as well as royal physician. In this plate from a 1773 reprint of his *Phalainologia nova* ... (1692), a study of whales from specimens washed up on the east Scottish coast, the bottom illustration is of a whale of the genus *Balaenoptera*, of which several species are named after him. Sibbald's long life was dogged by tragedy and personal injury; he was hit in the face by a golf club in 1690, and two years later had a bad fall from his horse after getting his spurs tangled.

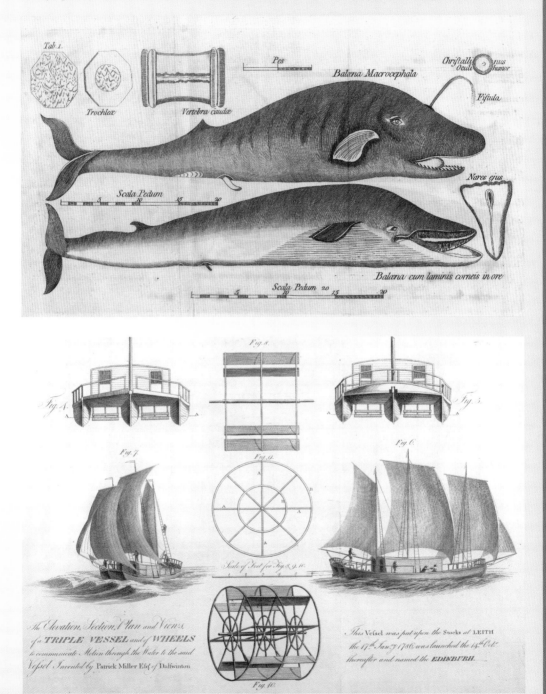

Above: Patrick Miller (1731–1815), a banker who owned estates near Dumfries, had a mechanical turn of mind. These illustrations by Alexander Nasmyth (1758–1840) are from a book Miller published in 1787, describing his invention of a trimaran, worked by hand-cranked paddles. The following year he sponsored, in collaboration with William Symington (1763–1831), the first voyage of a boat powered by steam, across Dalswinton Loch.

9. Broadsides and Chapbooks

Broadsides began in the 17th century as single sheets of paper printed on one side. For 300 years they provided an eager public with the kind of sensational reading offered today by the tabloid press. From royal proclamations and public notices, they became vehicles for political agitation and for popular culture such as ballads, songs, and accounts of executions and speeches from the scaffold.

Below: Heading of the broadside (price one penny) published in Edinburgh on the day of the execution in January 1829 of William Burke, the serial killer who, with his accomplice William Hare, supplied bodies for dissection.

EXECUTION.

A Full and True Account of the Last Speech and Dying Declaration of WILLIAM BURKE, who was Executed at Edinburgh this morning, for Murder, and his body given for dissection ; also of his conduct and behaviour since his condemnation, and on the Scaffold.

Edinburgh, 28th January, 1829.

morning, WILLIAM BURKE, the wretched ied so much of public attention since his of the unheard of atrocities disclosed at

ANNIE LAURIE.

Maxwelton braes are bonnie,
  Where early fa's the dew,
'Twas there that Annie Laurie,
  Gi'ed me her promise true.
Gi'ed me her promise true—
  Which ne'er forgot will be,
And for bonnie Annie Laurie
  I'd lay me down and dee.

Her brow is like the snaw-drift,
  Her neck is like the swan,
Her face it is the fairest
  That e'er the sun shone on.
That e'er the sun shone on—
  And dark blue is her e'e,
And for bonnie Annie Laurie
  I'd lay me down and dee.

Like dew on gowans lying,
  Is the fa' o' her fairy feet,
And like winds, in simmer sighing,
  Her voice is low and sweet.
Her voice is low and sweet—
  And she's a' the world to me ;
And for bonnie Annie Laurie
  I'd lay me down and dee.

Printed and Sold by JAMES LINDSAY, Wholesale Stationer, 9 King Street, (City) Glasgow. Upwards of 50,000 different sorts always on hand; also, a great variety of Pictures, Song-books, Histories &c. Shops and Hawkers

Left: The well-known song on this broadside of the 1850s was set to music by Alicia Anne Spottiswoode (1810–1900). The author was probably the Jacobite soldier, William Douglas of Fingland (1672–c. 1760). He had a romance with the much younger Anne Laurie (1682–1764), youngest daughter of Sir Robert Laurie of Maxwelton, though each finally married someone else. Spottiswoode added a third verse, and decorously replaced the sexual imagery in the first five lines of the second. The printer, James Lindsay, whose standard advertisement is at the foot, was a prolific supplier of popular literature. Woodcuts, usually used time and again to illustrate different texts, increased the marketing potential.

BRIDGE.

CHRISTMAS Time while mirth
    abounded,
  Thro' the country far and wide,
Happy homes are turned to sadness,
  Dear friends in death lay side by
    side by side
Young and old upon the railway,
  In that fatal train that day,
Little thought to death were going,
  From this life they've passed away.
      Refrain.
Tay Bridge gave way the train went
    hurling,
  Down into the deadly deep,
Just a crash and all was over,
  Many there in death now sleep.

Mothers with there little infants,
  Fathers sons and sweethearts true
Laugh'd and jok'd so free together,
  As along the rails they did pursue,
No thought of danger was among
    them,
  Thinking of old Chistmas cheer,
All was merry and light-hearted,
  Returning home they had no fear.

That Sabbath night while the storm
    was raging,
  The Edinburgh train went on its
    way,
Watch'd by a few who felt the danger
  As on Tay Bridge she steamed away
Sparks of fire they saw ascending.
  While down went crashing, bridge
    and train,
Into the river smash'd to pieces,
  Buried in the watery main.

At the railway stations friends were
    waiting,
  For the arrival of the train,
But when the news to them was bro-
    ken
  It filled their hearts with grief and
    pain,
Mothers cried "Give me my children"
  Fathers shed a silent tear,
Brothers, sisters, friends & sweethearts
  Wept for those they lov'd so dear.

Many now are sad and lonely,
  Thinking of a poor dear friend,
Little orphans now are weeping,
  For their parents fearful end,
None of us can tell the moment,
  When from this earth we'll have to
    go,
Those poor souls little thought of
    dying,
  In that fatal train below.

Above: Ballad of the 1879 Tay Bridge disaster, in which all 75 passengers died when the centre span of the bridge collapsed in hurricane-force winds.

Right: William Cameron (c. 1787–1851), nicknamed Hawkie, sold broadsides on the streets of Glasgow, buying for a penny from a local printer a dozen sheets, which he then sold for a halfpenny each. Out of his profits, he would go back and purchase a further dozen, several times on a good day, especially if there was an execution. He was a great character, with a ready wit and the ability to compose his own songs. His autobiography was published posthumously in 1888.

The chapbook, a small paperback with self-cover, usually printed on both sides of a single sheet or part-sheet and folded into eight, 12, 16, or 24 pages, vied in popularity with the broadside. Often illustrated with woodcuts which bore little or no relation to the text, chapbooks were cheaply printed on poor paper, and were sold for a penny each by itinerant salesmen, or chapmen. It is estimated that between the 17th and 19th centuries about 15,000 titles were printed in 33 different centres in Scotland: in Fintray, Newton Stewart, and Inveraray, for example, as well as in Aberdeen, Edinburgh, Glasgow, Falkirk, and Stirling. They covered subjects from sermons to songs, poems to potted biographies and prophecies, legends to last words of those on the scaffold, and adult education manuals to almanacs, with a few children's items.

Below: Typical chapbook of 24 pages, 17 cm high. It is attributed to Dougal Graham and published in Glasgow by James Lumsden (1752/3–1821), a wholesale stationer who also published children's books.

Above: If only half the chapbooks attributed to Dougal Graham (?1721–1779) were really written by him, he was the best-selling author in Scotland in the 18th century, such was the size of the business. Hunchbacked, with a crippled leg, and under 5 feet tall, he was appointed town-crier of Glasgow in about 1770. He accompanied the Jacobite army in 1745/6, and wrote a racy account in verse of the campaign (1746): a third edition (1774) included the adventures of Charles Edward Stuart after Culloden.

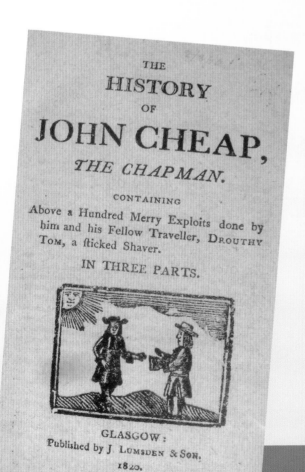

THE
HISTORY
OF
JOHN CHEAP,
THE CHAPMAN.

CONTAINING

Above a Hundred Merry Exploits done by him and his Fellow Traveller, DROUTHY TOM, a sticked Shaver.

IN THREE PARTS.

GLASGOW:
Published by J. LUMSDEN & SON.
1820.

10. Bookselling and Publishing

Whereas the printer had often shouldered the responsibility of financing the whole operation and distributing the books, the 18th century saw the rise of the specialist bookseller and the bookseller/publisher. In the wake of the Act of Union of 1707, marketing arrangements were made between Scottish and English publishers and booksellers. Businesses run by Scots were established in London, such as those of Andrew Millar (1705–68), and of William Strahan (1715–85) and his English partner, Thomas Cadell (1742–1802), who had been apprenticed to Millar. Emigration was a factor in developing overseas markets, with reprints of Scottish books being published by Scottish immigrants in Philadelphia and to a lesser extent in Dublin.

The effect on the diffusion of literature and on authors' earnings of the two significant 18th-century pieces of copyright legislation, the Act of Anne 1710 and the House of Lords' decision in the case of *Donaldson v. Becket* (22 February 1774), neither of which applied in America or Ireland, may, however, have been exaggerated. Copyright allows the owners control over their intellectual property for whatever time is specified. Under the 1710 act, to which Scottish booksellers subscribed, copyright in works already published was assured to the present owner (whether author or bookseller) for a further 28 years from 1710. Not so English booksellers, who held that, under the Common Law for property, works that they had bought outright from authors, sometimes for large sums, remained theirs in perpetuity.

Below: A reconstruction by the painter William Borthwick Johnstone (1804–68) of the circulating library owned by James Sibbald (1747–1803), as it would have been in 1786/7. Sibbald himself is in the background, taking down a book while he talks to Lord Monboddo, philosopher, judge, and celebrated eccentric, whose daughter Eliza Burnett is the languid lady seated. She was much admired by Robert Burns (second from left), who wrote an elegy, with which he was dissatisfied, on her death in 1790 from consumption at the age of 24. On the far right is a young Walter Scott, who, in his memoir of his early years, describes catching at Sibbald's his first sight of Burns, the 'boast of Scotland'.

(Edinburgh Booksellers' Society)

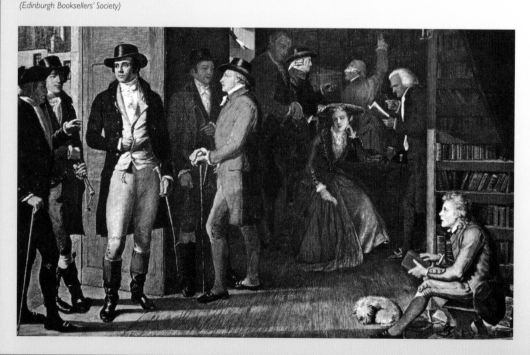

The impasse lasted 65 years. It was broken by an Edinburgh bookseller, Alexander Donaldson (1726/7–1794), who had opened a business in London in 1763 and had ever since been flooding the market legitimately with cheap reprints. In 1768, however, he printed in Edinburgh a cheap edition of *The Seasons*, by the Scottish poet James Thomson (1700–48), first published in 1730, the copyright of which, under the 1710 act, had expired in 1758. Thomas Becket served an injunction on him, believing that he had bought the perpetual copyright from the executors of Andrew Millar, who had purchased it on that apparent basis from Thomson. In a historic ruling, the Lords finally threw out Becket's case, and upheld the precedence of the act of 1710. The principles of this ruling still apply today to international copyright.

Left: Engraving by W. Forrest of the High Street, Edinburgh in the mid-18th century. The east end of the Luckenbooths (centre, facing) was a prime commercial site. Its ground floor was occupied from 1773 to 1815 by the influential bookseller/publisher, William Creech (1745–1815), who would stand among the crowd in the doorway with his 'black silk breeches and powdered head'. In the flat above, Allan Ramsay established his library in 1725.

Left: William Blackwood (1776–1834) established his business in 1804. He founded the *Edinburgh Monthly Magazine* (1817) as a Tory rival to the Whig-orientated *Edinburgh Review*; it was renamed Blackwood's *Edinburgh Magazine* in October 1817. The firm of William Blackwood and Sons became one of the leading literary publishers of the 19th century. *(SNPG)*

Developments in the Scottish book trade coincided with the Scottish Enlightenment, a modern term for the extraordinary burgeoning of cultural talents between the Glorious Revolution of 1688 and the death of Sir Walter Scott in 1832.

11. Figures of the Scottish Enlightenment

Left: **Robert Burns** (1759–96) is one of the few major poets in any language to have overcome an indigent upbringing. Faced with financial and personal problems, he managed in 1786 to raise money from subscribers to have *Poems, Chiefly in the Scottish Dialect* printed in Kilmarnock: it made his name and changed his life. His poetical range was extraordinary, and he wrote equally well in English and Scots, which he developed as a language of poetry. *(SNPG: artist Alexander Naysmith)*

Right: **Archibald Constable** (1774–1827) acquired the *Scots Magazine* (founded 1739) in 1801, established the *Edinburgh Review* (1802), and published the *Edinburgh Philosophical Journal* from its inception in 1819. Two potentially profitable investments, the purchase in 1812 of the rights and stock of the *Encyclopaedia Britannica* and the publication of the works of Walter Scott, contributed to his ruin in 1826, when the London agents of the encyclopaedia collapsed, and Scott and his printer were declared bankrupt. *(SNPG: artist Andrew Geddes)*

Left: **Susan Ferrier** (1782–1854), youngest of ten children, began to write a novel while managing her father's household. It was published anonymously in Edinburgh as *Marriage* (1818), as were *The Inheritance* (1824) and *Destiny* (1831). Only in 1850 did she allow her authorship to be recognised, having apparently been reluctant to be associated with a form of writing whose wit, shrewd observation, and social comment appealed to a broad readership. *(SNPG: artist Augustin Edouart)*

Right: **James Hogg** (1770–1835), known from his calling as the 'Ettrick Shepherd', had little education beyond Border ballads and folklore, which he used in collaborating with Scott on Volume Two of *Minstrelsy of the Scottish Border* (1802). He wrote good verse, including *The Queen's Wake* (1813), lively journalism in *Blackwood's Edinburgh Magazine* (1817–30), and four novels, ignored or reviled in his lifetime, of which *The Private Memoirs and Confessions of a Justified Sinner* (1824), a psychological account of possession, is held to be one of the finest novels in the Scottish tradition.

Left: **David Hume** (1711–76) is regarded as one of the greatest 18th-century philosophers. In frugal seclusion in France, while recovering from a nervous breakdown, he wrote *A Treatise of Human Nature* (1739–40). It was not well received, but he persevered with *Essays Moral and Political* (1741–42). His dismissal of religion in his writings cost him professorships at Edinburgh and Glasgow universities. *An Enquiry Concerning Human Understanding* was first published in 1748 as *Philosophical Essays Concerning Human Understanding*: he refused to have *Dialogues Concerning Natural Religion* (1779) published during his lifetime.

Right: **Francis Hutcheson** (1694–1746), Ulster-born philospher, had already published in Dublin *An Inquiry into the Original of our Ideas of Beauty and Virtue* (1725) when in 1730 he became professor of moral philosophy at Glasgow University, where he was the first to teach the subject in English, not Latin. His lectures and the posthumously published *A System of Moral Philosophy* (1755), whose central theme was happiness, strongly influenced the thinking of the Scottish Enlightenment. *(SNPG: artist Antonio Selvi)*

Alexander MacDonald (Alasdair Mac Mhaighstir Alasdair) (c. 1695 – c.1770), Gaelic poet, was a teacher when in 1741 his vocabulary was the first secular book in Gaelic to be printed. He converted to Roman Catholicism in 1745, and played a prominent role in the campaign of Charles Edward Stuart, whose Gaelic tutor he was. The collection of his poems published in 1751, the first printed book of secular Gaelic verse, contained so many anti-government sentiments that it is said it was burned in Edinburgh by the public hangman. His wide-ranging verse includes 'Birlinn chlann Raghnaill' (Galley of Clanranald), an outstanding sea poem.

Left: **James Macpherson** (1736–96) perpetrated a series of literary forgeries which profoundly influenced the European Romantic movement. After publishing in 1760 what he claimed were translations of fragments of ancient Gaelic verse, he was commissioned by the literary establishment further to investigate the oral tradition. He obliged with *Fingal* (1761) and *Temora* (1763), his own 'translations' of epics purporting to be by Ossian, a 3rd-century Gaelic warrior poet, son of the legendary Fingal. Their success at the time, and later, was largely due to the fact that many people wanted them to be authentic. *(SNPG)*

Right: **Allan Ramsay** (1684–1758), poet and dramatist, wrote in both English and Scots, which had fallen into disuse as a medium of poetry since James VI took his court to London in 1603. A former master wig-maker, he published his *Poems* (1721) and anthologies of ballads and songs (1724 and 1724–37), which further revived public interest in Scottish literature. His verse play, *The Gentle Shepherd* (1725), was the first notable Scottish drama for almost 200 years. In 1725 he founded the first circulating library in Britain. *(SNPG: artist William Aikman)*

Left: **(Sir) Walter Scott** (1771–1832), novelist, poet, short-story writer, historian, and folklorist, began his prodigious writing career with ballad-epics in the Romantic tradition: *The Lay of the Last Minstrel* (1805), *Marmion* (1808), and *The Lady of the Lake* (1810). They were printed by James Ballantyne (1772–1833), and their success was a factor in Scott lending him money, and becoming a partner in the business. With *Waverley* (1814), Scott began a line of enormously popular historical novels, until 1827 published anonymously. This was probably because, as sheriff-depute of Selkirkshire since 1799, he did not want to appear to be leading several lives. Ballantyne's business collapsed in 1826, and Scott was declared bankrupt to the tune of £100,000. In spite of recurring illness, he refused his friends' financial help, and for the rest of his life wrote unceasingly to repay his debts. His stage-management of the visit to Edinburgh of George IV, for which he received a baronetcy, initiated the Scottish tartan revival. *(SNPG: artist David Wilkie)*

Left: **Adam Smith** (1723–90), political economist, was influenced by the thinking of Francis Hutcheson, whom he followed at one remove as professor of moral philosophy at Glasgow University 1752–64. In *The Theory of Moral Sentiments* (1759), he aimed to explain individual behaviour and its effect upon society. In retirement in Kirkcaldy, he wrote *An inquiry into the nature and causes of the wealth of nations* (1776), printed in London for Strahan and Cadell, a work of great international influence in which he examined the forces contributing to world development. *(SNPG: artist James Tassie)*

12. Machinery for Printing

Letterpress is printing from raised type or blocks. With certain minimal improvements, the basic wooden press remained in use for over 200 years. In 1800 it was superseded by an iron press invented by Earl Stanhope (1753–1816), which increased the pressure and required less effort to operate. At a maximum of 250 impressions an hour, it was not much faster than the wooden press, but its efficacy was such that *The Times* immediately ordered enough machines to fulfil its daily commitments. Stanhope declined to patent his invention, to allow the industry to make full use of it. In Scotland, the *Glasgow Herald*, producing two four-page issues a week with a circulation of 2,500, also changed its presses, to an American version, the Columbian, on which it was said two strong operators could turn out 350 impressions an hour. *The Times* switched to steam-driven presses in 1814, the *Glasgow Herald* not until 1851.

With the steam press came also the invention of a method of printing both sides of the sheet in the same pass, known as perfecting.

Below: Steam-driven perfector of about 1820, issuing between 800 and 1,000 sheets an hour, printed on both sides. The paper (top left) is printed on one side by the adjacent cylinder, passes over the smaller cylinders, and is printed on the other side before being delivered into the hands of the operator sitting in the middle of the machine. The type for the second side is flat on the table to the right, where it is inked by rollers.

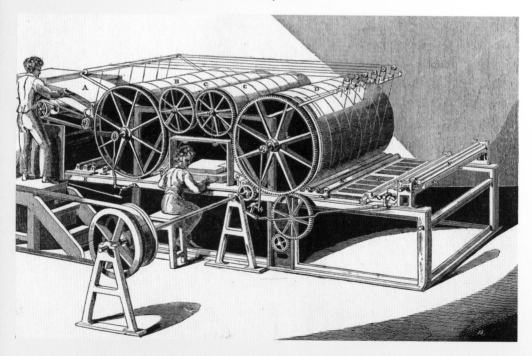

Stanhope was also involved in the re-invention of printing by stereotype, the patent for which he purchased from Andrew Foulis and another Scot, Alexander Tilloch (1759–1825), who had developed their own method of making the plates. The introduction of the curved stereo, patented in France in 1844, enabled the plate to be attached to the cylinder of a rotary press, thus vastly increasing the speed of printing.

Right: Thomas Nelson junior (1822–92), second son of the founder of the Edinburgh firm of publishers and printers, Thomas Nelson, exhibited this press at the Great Exhibition in 1851. Its significance lies in its pioneering combination of features: steam-driven (the flywheel is on the right), it is a reel-fed, rotary, perfecting machine, incorporating a serrated cutter, and printing 10,000 sheets an hour. Like Stanhope, Nelson declined to patent his invention, which in due course was recognised as the forerunner of the 20th-century newspaper press. This particular machine spent the duration of World War I in the hands of the Germans in Leipzig, having been lent for an exhibition there. It was returned to Edinburgh at the end of the war, in perfect working condition. Minus its sheeter (cutting device), it has been in the National Museum of Scotland since 1980.

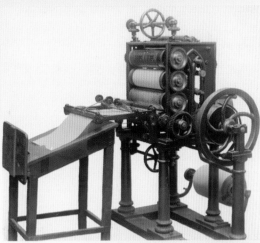

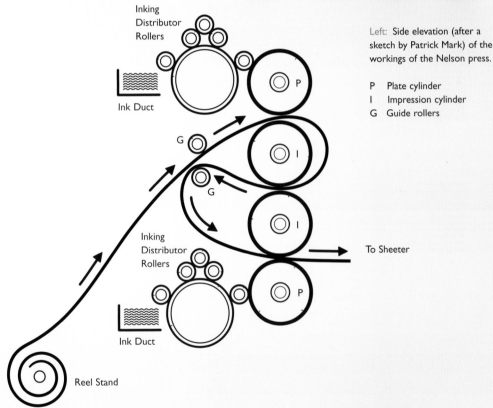

Inking Distributor Rollers

Ink Duct

G

G

P

I

I

Inking Distributor Rollers

Ink Duct

P

To Sheeter

Reel Stand

Left: Side elevation (after a sketch by Patrick Mark) of the workings of the Nelson press.

P   Plate cylinder
I   Impression cylinder
G   Guide rollers

An average hand-compositor could assemble about 1,000 letters and spaces an hour: at that rate, it would have taken one person, working an eight-hour day, almost five months to set up the type for Sir Walter Scott's three-volume *Waverley*, or seven times longer than it took the author to write volumes Two and Three. To match the speed with which the new presses could operate, it was necessary, especially for newspaper work, to mechanise typesetting. The problem was finally resolved by Ottmar Mergenthaler in the USA in 1886, with a composite machine which produced from molten metal a solid line of type (or slug), properly justified, and ejected it into a tray, or galley. After printing, the slugs were returned to the machine and melted down, for use again. The Linotype could produce between 6,000 and 10,000 characters an hour, depending on the skill of the operator.

Left: Mergenthaler's 1890 Linotype machine, of a kind which was employed by the *Glasgow Herald* until 1980, when the change was made to typesetting by computer.

Book printers in Europe, however, generally decried the Linotype as unable to reflect typographical niceties, and it was not until 1901 that another American invention, the Monotype, was available in Britain. This was not so much a machine as two machines: the first, with a keyboard operator, delivered a spool of paper punched with perforations indicating the various characters, and the second cast lines of type in hot metal in which each character was separate, and could subsequently be corrected by hand.

Alongside the development of photography went the invention of a method of printing photographs. A glass screen hatched with fine crossed lines was interposed between the image and the negative onto which it was being projected. This broke up the image into tiny dots, the same distance apart but varying in size according to the intensity of the tone. The result, when printed from a halftone block made from the screened negative, reproduced the gradation of tones of the original.

The resemblance to full colour was achieved in the 1890s, partly due to the discoveries in colour vision and optics made by the Scottish physicist, James Clerk Maxwell (1831–79). Separate halftone plates were made from negatives filtered to produce the colours magenta, cyan, and yellow, to which was later added a black plate to achieve depth. These were then printed one after the other.

The basic principle of lithographic printing is that oil-based inks and water do not mix. The process was invented in Germany in 1798, and came to Scotland in about 1815. In its most basic form, a design is drawn in reverse on a limestone slab (or stone) in greasy ink or with a grease pencil. The porous stone is then damped with water, which does not adhere to the design. The damp areas reject the printing ink, which is, however, accepted by the greasy lines of the design. By this method, tones can readily be reproduced.

In 1870, the number of lithographic printing businesses involved mainly in jobbing work was about 122 in Glasgow, and 60 in Edinburgh. Between 1869 and 1889, five women are listed as professional lithographic printers, in Aberdeen, Edinburgh, Glasgow, Kirkcaldy, and Paisley respectively.

The application of lithography to book printing was achieved by the development of zinc plates on which the printing image of type and illustrations could be reproduced by photography. The plates could also be wrapped round the cylinder of a rotary press. To be able to print evenly on different kinds of paper, and integrate pictures and text, the machine used three cylinders: the plate cylinder, damped and then inked by rollers, transferred (or offset) the image onto a second cylinder covered with a rubber blanket, from which the image was printed onto paper carried by a third cylinder. The principles survive today; the process is known as offset litho (or just offset). A web-offset machine is one fed from a roll of paper.

Below: **Sheet-fed offset litho press**

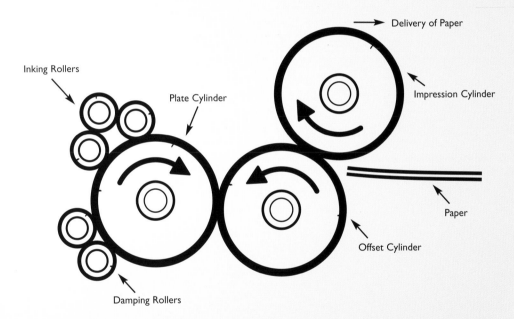

Delivery of Paper

Inking Rollers

Plate Cylinder

Impression Cylinder

Offset Cylinder

Paper

Damping Rollers

To meet the expansion of the newspaper industry and the growing need for educational books and writing materials as well as for Bibles and literary works, there were at the end of the 18th century about 416 paper mills in England and Wales, and 49 in Scotland, all manufacturing paper by hand. In 1803, two Scottish mills are recorded as having installed steam engines to assist parts of the operation. The process was revolutionised, however, by the Fourdrinier machine, named after two brothers, partners in a stationery firm, who financed the development in Britain of a French invention. The design and engineering work was done by Bryan Donkin (1768–1855), who introduced numerous improvements and became a wealthy man. The first Fourdrinier machine to be installed in Scotland was at Culter, Aberdeenshire, in 1811. The Fourdrinier brothers themselves, however, had been declared bankrupt in 1810. Henry (1766–1854), the elder, died in poverty, having lived to see the explosion of the market for cheap newspapers and books, made possible in part by his original initiative and investment.

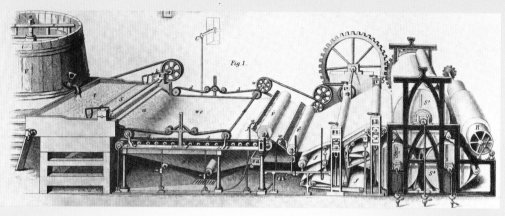

Above: A Fourdrinier machine of between 1830 and 1850, the principles of which still apply to paper manufacture today. The raw material, in liquid form, flows from the vat (far left) onto a moving belt of wire mesh, through which the water drains. The fibres then pass between two sets of wet press rollers, and onto and through three steam-heated drying cylinders, before emerging and being reeled up.

Had things turned out differently, there might have been permanent Scottish input into the industry. Robert Cameron invented in 1816 a machine with a novel feature, introducing steam into the pressing rollers as a drying element. It seems, however, only to have been installed in mills at Polton (Midlothian) and Bucksburn (Aberdeen). The Bertram brothers, George, William, and James, of Sciennes, Edinburgh, were in the 1850s and 1860s making and supplying paper-making machines to the industry world wide. In 1862, George exhibited at the International Machinery Exhibition a machine with eight drying cylinders, producing a roll 80 inches wide.

It has been calculated that between 1508, the beginning of printing in Scotland, and 1800, presses were set up in 33 Scottish towns and villages. The spread of literacy as well as the population growth meant a greater reading public, and during the 19th century the number of printing centres in Scotland increased by 400 per cent, to 198. The consequence of an expanding market, allied to mechanical advances in printing and paper-making techniques, and greater competition, was lower unit costs of production, and thus lower prices.

Some printers' terms

chapel   An association of craftsmen in a printing house.

copy   Any matter to be reproduced in type.

face   A particular design of type, e.g. Times New Roman.

film   Photographic film in positive or negative form from which printing plates can be made.

forme   Type matter or type and blocks imposed and secured in the chase for printing.

fount   (US **font**) A complete set of type of a particular design and size.

imposition Arrangement of pages for printing so that they will read consecutively when the sheet is folded.

literal   (US **typo**) Typesetting error.

roman   Ordinary type, as distinct from *italic* or **bold**.

wayzgoose An annual printers' outing.

widow   Short last line of a paragraph appearing as the first line on a page.

13. Plays and Poetry

Allan Ramsay's verse play, *The Gentle Shepherd*, was first printed by Thomas Ruddiman in 1725; metamorphosed into a ballad opera, it was performed in 1729 in Edinburgh by pupils of Haddington Grammar School. Subsequently it was the most popular pastoral comedy in 18th-century Britain. In 1736 Ramsay opened a theatre with a permanent company in Carruber's Close, Edinburgh, an ominous address, since the 1737 Licensing Act banning stage plays outside London, strongly upheld by the local council with vehement clerical support, forced its closure.

Above: One of five engravings from a 1798 edition of *The Gentle Shepherd*, printed in Edinburgh.

Ramsay was probably instrumental in the opening in 1747 of the Canongate Concert Hall, where plays could still be put on as free extensions to a genuine concert. Under this guise in 1756, *Douglas*, a romantic tragedy by John Home (1722–1808) with strong nationalistic undertones, was performed, sparking off the most sensational uproar in Scottish theatrical history. The literary establishment and the playgoers loved it, but Home was a minister of the Church, and other ministers were in the audience. The Presbytery of Edinburgh reacted with outrage. Home was forced to resign his parish, and ministers who had seen the play were admonished or suspended for immorality. *Douglas* was published in 1757 in Dublin, and anonymously in Edinburgh and London, where it played at the Theatre Royal, Covent Garden.

Right: Heading of the playbill advertising the second night of *Douglas*, as a gratis addition to a concert, to get round the 1737 act. Only in 1767 was a patent granted to the new Edinburgh Theatre Royal.

SECOND NIGHT.
THEATRE Canongate,
THIS EVENING,
Being 15th DECEMBER 1756,
A CONCERT OF MUSIC.
After which will be presented (*gratis*)
The NEW TRAGEDY
DOUGLAS.
Taken from an Ancient *SCOTS STORY*,
AND
Writ by a GENTLEMAN of SCOTLAND.

Also published anonymously, but for reasons of modesty, were the early poetry and plays of Joanna Baillie (1762–1851). After her *De Montfort* opened at Drury Lane in 1800, its author was revealed not to be Walter Scott or John Philip Kemble, as had been thought, but a douce Scottish spinster living in London with her doctor brother. Her commentaries and vision were more incisive than her stagecraft, but she enjoyed great esteem. The most frequently performed of her plays, *The Family Legend* (1810), was heavily edited by Scott, who produced it for the stage in Edinburgh, where it was also printed by James Ballantyne.

Left: Scott's *Rob Roy* was adapted for the stage so many times that there was a theatrical adage: 'When in doubt, play *Rob Roy*.' This engraving of the notable actor Charles Mackay (1787–1857) comes from a treatment by Isaac Pocock (1782–1835), published in 1822. When he appeared at the Glasgow Prince's Theatre Royal in 1852, Mackay was said to be performing Bailie Nicol Jarvie for the 1,134th time.

Two Scots, J. M. Barrie (1860–1937) and James Bridie, pseudonym of
O. H. Mavor (1888–1951), dominated the London stage of their times.
Two others, who wrote largely in Scots, the former miner Joe Corrie
(1894–1968), with gritty realism, and Robert McLellan (1907–85), with
historical insights, influenced particularly the development of the
amateur theatre in Scotland.

Right: In our own times, Liz Lochhead (b.1947), herself a stage director and performer, has
published both plays and poems in Scotland, as well as her own translation into Scots of
Molière's *Tartuffe* (1985). *(Photo Gordon Wright)*

What has been called the Scottish Renaissance was effectively launched by Christopher Murray
Grieve (1892–1978) with the publication (by the firm of Blackwood) of two books of verse
containing poems in Scots which he attributed to a friend called Hugh MacDiarmid: *Sangschaw*
(1925) and *Penny Wheep* (1926). Hugh MacDiarmid became his permanent pseudonym, and the
Lowland Scots which he employed was a composite version from different dialects. He used it again
in *A Drunk Man Looks at the Thistle* (1926), a sustained study of national and personal
introspection, as well as a fine lyrical poem.

MacDiarmid was helped in his translations of Gaelic poetry by Sorley MacLean (Somhairle
MacGill-Eain) (1911–96), whose first collection, *Dàin do Eimhir agus dàin eile* (1943), reflected a
tormented love affair and his remorse at not fighting in the Spanish Civil War. Though he had a
first-class degree in English, MacLean chose to write in Gaelic, denying himself a wide readership
but creating a modern poetry in an ancient tongue.

Below: Page from MacLean's *Dàin do Eimhir agus dàin eile* (left) and the matching one from *Poems to Eimhir* (1971), the
English translation by Iain Crichton Smith (Iain Mac a'Ghobhainn) (1928–98), poet and novelist in English and Gaelic.

III.

Cha do chuir de bhuaireadh riamh
no thrioblaid dhian 'nam chré
allaban Chriosda air an talamh
no muillionan nan speur.

'S cha d' ghabh mi suim de aisling bhaoith —
coille uaine tìr an sgeòil —
mar leum mo chridhe rag ri tuar
a gàire 's cuailein òir.

Agus chuir a h-àilleachd sgleò
air bochdainn 's air creuchd sheirbh
agus air saoghal tuigse Leninn,
air fhoighidinn 's air fheirg.

IV.

A nighean a' chùil bhuidhe, throm-bhuidh, òr-bhuidh,
fonn do bheòil-sa 's gaoir na h-Eòrpa,
a nighean gheal chasurlach aighearach bhòidheach
cha bhiodh masladh ar latha-ne searbh 'nad phòig-sa.

An tugadh d' fhonn no t' àilleachd ghlòrmhor
bhuam-sa gràinealachd mharbh nan dòigh so,
a' bhrùid 's am mèirleach air ceann na h-Eòrpa
's do bheul-sa, uaill-dhearg, 's an t-sean òran?

An tugadh corp geal is clàr gréine
bhuam-sa cealgaireachd dhubh na bréine,
nimh bhùirdeasach is puinnsean créide
is diblidheachd ar n-Albann éitigh?

An cuireadh bòidhichead is ceòl suaimhneach
bhuam-sa breòiteachd an aobhair bhuain so,
am mèinear Spàinnteach a' leum ri cruadal
is 'anam mórail 'dol sìos gun bhruaillean?

Dé bhiodh pòg do bheòil uaibhrich
mar ris gach braon de 'n fhuil luachmhoir
a thuit air raointean reòta, fuara
nam beann Spàinnteach bho fhòirne cruadhach?

Dé gach cuach de d' chual òr-bhuidh
ris gach bochdainn, àmhghar 's dòrainn
a thig 's a thàinig air sluagh na h-Eòrpa
bho Long nan Daoine gu daors' a' mhór-shluaigh?

IV

Girl of the yellow, heavy-yellow, gold-yellow hair,
the tune of your lips and Europe's pain together.
Lustrous, ringletted, joyful, beautiful lass,
our time's shame would not infect your kiss.

Can the music of your beauty hide from me
the ominous discord in this harmony?
The rampant thief and brute at Europe's head,
the ancient songs, your lips so proud and red.

Can a body's whiteness and a forehead's sun
conceal that impudent treachery from my brain—
spite of the bourgeoisie, poison of its creed,
a dismal Scotland, feeble and weak-kneed?

Can beauty and the mendacity of verse
deceive the patient with its transient cures
or hide the Spanish miner from his doom,
his soul going down without delirium?

What is your kiss, electrical and proud,
when valued by each drop of precious blood
that fell on the frozen mountain-sides of Spain
when men were dying in their bitter pain?

What is each ringlet of your golden hair
when weighed against that poverty and fear
which Europe's people bear and still must bear
from the first slave-ship to slavery entire?

20

14. Reading for Everyone

The dynastic contribution of Scotland to the British and international book trades has been remarkable. It is especially so when one considers that the founder in 1768 of the historic publishing house of John Murray was born John McMurray in Edinburgh, and that Daniel Macmillan (1813–57) and his brother Alexander (1818–96), who established the firm of Macmillan, were also Scottish.

Of imprints which remained under family control until the latter years of the 20th century, William Blackwood was, as we have seen, established in 1804, and became William Blackwood and Sons in 1835; Adam Black (1784–1874) founded in 1807 the business that became A. & C. Black; John Blackie (1782–1874) was publishing by 1809, and Thomas Nelson (1780–1861) by 1818; the brothers William (1800–83) and Robert Chambers (1802–71), both also authors of note, founded W. & R. Chambers in 1819; in that same year, a young evangelist called William Collins (1789–1853) set up the business which, between then and 1979, had six consecutive William Collinses in charge; and in 1826, John Bartholomew Snr (1805–61) founded the firm of mapmakers which remained in the family until 1980. In 1848, James Thin (1824–1915) bought up the stock and fittings of a failed bookseller in Infirmary Street, Edinburgh, and set up on his own. The family firm of James Thin, Booksellers, became the leading academic bookseller in Scotland, until going into voluntary administration in 2002.

Blackie (until 1967), Collins (until 1993), and Nelson (until 1966) were also in the forefront of Scottish book printers, as was R. & R. Clark, founded in 1846 by Robert Clark (1825–94). London publishers used Clark to print quality editions of popular authors such as R. L. Stevenson, Hardy, Compton Mackenzie, Kipling, and George Bernard Shaw.

Below: Extract from *The Gospel by St John* (1834), in an embossed type design pioneered by the Edinburgh publisher James Gall (c. 1784–1874) for the blind. The system had been employed in Paris since 1786, but Gall improved its effectiveness by means of a typeface that avoided curves. He was deeply concerned about the needs of the blind: a royal commission report (1852) observed, 'It is to Mr Gall, perhaps, more than any other man, that the interest in education of the blind was awakened throughout Great Britain and America.' The Braille system was not introduced into Britain until 1869.

During the 19th century the population of Edinburgh grew from 62,000 to 350,000, and of Glasgow from 77,000 to 760,000. The education acts of 1870 (England and Wales) and 1872 (Scotland), which made elementary education compulsory, increased the need not only for schoolbooks but for reading matter for those for whom the ability to read was a means to an end, not the end itself. The Chambers brothers met the growing demand for popular learning with *Chambers's Encyclopaedia* (1860–68) in ten volumes (520 parts); *Chambers's Edinburgh Journal*, established in 1832, was published weekly until 1897, and then monthly until 1956.

Robert Chambers's *Vestiges of the Natural History of Creation* (1844) was published anonymously in London, because he did not want the expected furore to damage his literary reputation or that of his firm. His exposition prepared the ground for Charles Darwin and others to present similar views on evolution.

Blackie, Collins, and Nelson were in the vanguard of the educational revolution; all three went in a big way into schoolbooks for the home and overseas markets, and children's books designed initially as school prizes. Nelson also developed several series of well-produced and tastefully-bound classics at sixpence or sevenpence each. The first Nelson 'Sevenpenny' was issued on 15 May 1907, followed three days later by the first 'Sevenpenny' from Collins, who also published a 'Penny library' for schools. Collins 'Pocket classics' had begun to appear in 1903 at one shilling each. The linchpin of the Collins publishing and printing operations, however, was the Bible, in many forms: by 1860 William Collins had in print 17 editions of the complete work, in about 300 different styles of binding.

Margaret Oliphant (1828–97) was probably the first Scottish novelist since Scott to achieve popular fame, but her life, during which she wrote almost 100 novels, 50 short stories, and innumerable non-fiction works, articles, and reviews, was a catalogue of periodic misery, unrelenting toil, and little profit. 'The Chronicles of Carlingford' (1861–76), a series of domestic novels set in England, was first serialised and then published in volume form by John Blackwood (1818–79), who also published all but one of the major novels of George Eliot (1819–80).

Right: *Up the Country* (1928) was the first in a sequence of novels covering the pioneering days by the Australian author Miles Franklin (1879–1954), writing as Brent of Bin Bin, an identity she refused to acknowledge until just before her death. Blackwood had also published her first book, *My Brilliant Career* (1901), regarded as the first genuine Australian novel, but it generated so much controversy that she withdrew it in 1910.

Nelson's literary adviser from 1907 to 1929 was John Buchan (1875–1940), a man of extraordinary literary industry who took on the job to finance his marriage. With assistance, he wrote for the firm the 24 volumes of Nelson's history of World War I, published fortnightly from February 1915 to July 1919 in issues of about 50,000 words each. To his friend and fellow-director, Thomas Arthur Nelson (1877–1917), he dedicated his most enduring thriller, *The Thirty-nine Steps*, published by Blackwood in 1915. As Lord Tweedsmuir of Elsfield, Buchan was Governor General of Canada from 1935 until his death.

Left: Neil Munro (1863–1930), journalist and writer of historical adventures and stories bordering on the Celtic Twilight genre, is best remembered for the richly comic tales and sketches about Para Handy and his Clyde puffer. Conceived as journalistic pieces, they were first published in book form by Blackwood in 1906, under the pseudonym of Hugh Foulis.

The first genuine Scottish newspaper was *Mercurius Caledonius*, with the issue for 31 December 1660 to 8 January 1661; before that newspapers printed in Scotland were reprints of London papers. The oldest surviving newspaper is the *Press and Journal*, established as *Aberdeen's Journal* in 1747. The *Herald* began in 1783 as the *Glasgow Advertiser*, followed 34 years later by the *Scotsman*. The [Dundee] *Courier* was first published in 1817. More recent survivors are the *Daily Record* (1895), *Sunday Post* (1915), *Scotland on Sunday* (1988), and the *Sunday Herald* (1999).

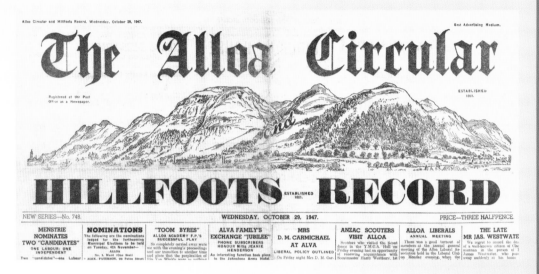

Above: Striking 1947 masthead, with a view of the Ochils, of a local newspaper established in 1869 and published in various guises until 1976. A rival publication, the *Alloa and Hillfoots Advertiser*, was founded as a monthly in 1841 and has been a weekly since 1855; it is now published in Dunfermline and printed in Glasgow. There are today about 100 local papers in Scotland with a combined circulation of nearly a million.

Right: Cover for the 1951 annual of the Broons. The Broon family and the comic strip of that other Scottish institution, Oor Wullie, made their first appearance in the issue of 8 March 1936 of the *Sunday Post*, published by D. C. Thomson of Dundee (established 1905). They were drawn by Dudley D. Watkins (1907–69), a member of the Thomson permanent stable of illustrators. The Broons and Oor Wullie still carry on today. Thomson had previously published adventure stories for boys in the *Rover, Wizard*, and *Hotspur*; in 1937 the firm launched the *Dandy*, the world's longest-running comic, which was followed in 1938 by the *Beano*.

(© D. C. Thomson Ltd)

The story of the book industry in Scotland over 500 years is one largely of survival and revival. There are today 71 full members of Publishing Scotland (formerly the Scottish Publishers Association), and certainly more books of Scottish interest are being published than, say, 30 years ago. The computer has completely revolutionised the origination and preparation of material for the press, and now digital printing is having a further fundamental effect on the economics of book production, making print on demand a viable option.

Notable Scottish survivors include the specialist book printer Bell and Bain (founded in 1831), the book binder Hunter and Foulis (1857), and seven university bookshops under the banner of John Smith and Son (1751), whose claim to be Glasgow's 'second oldest trading company and the oldest bookselling company in the English-speaking world' is probably correct.

Below left: Though Irvine Welsh's iconic first novel, *Trainspotting* (1993), was published in London, four chapters were issued in pamphlet format by Clocktower Press, South Queensferry, in 1992 under the title of *Past Tense*. *(Clocktower Press)*
Below right: The shape of things to come? This football quiz book (2006) incorporates a free CD, featuring clips from the radio programme on which it is based. *(Birlinn Ltd.)*

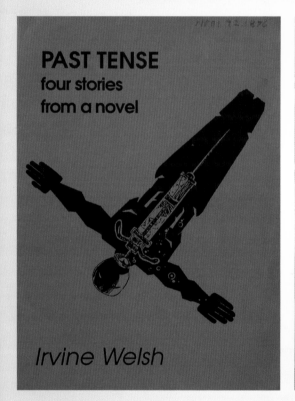

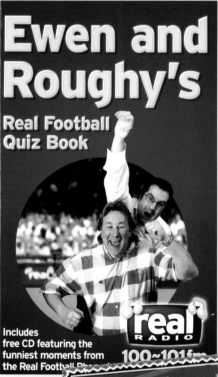

Amazon has changed the way many of us buy books, but there are in Edinburgh four major bookshops within walking distance of each other. Edinburgh itself, for its associations and general literary vitality, is the first UNESCO City of Literature. Three Scottish authors (Alexander McCall Smith, Ian Rankin, and Irvine Welsh) and one permanent resident (J. K. Rowling) are in the top flight of international best sellers, and Alexander McCall Smith remains, for the initial hardcover editions of his novels, faithful to the Scottish publisher who nurtured them.

Timeline

1314	Battle of Bannockburn.
1352–55	Barbour writes the *Bruce*.
c. 1460	Robert Henryson, *The Morall Fabillis*.
c. 1477	Blind Harry's *Wallace*.
1488–1513	Reign of James IV.
1507	Chepman and Myllar set up a press in Edinburgh under royal licence.
1508	The first Scottish printed books.
1513	Gavin Douglas writes his *Aeneid*.
1542	Thomas Davidson produces in Edinburgh the first printed acts of parliament.
1552	First printing in St Andrews, by John Scot.
1567	Abdication of Mary, Queen of Scots. The book of Common Order is the first book printed in Gaelic.
1567–1625	Reign of James VI.
1571	First printing in Stirling, by Robert Lekpreuik.
1579	First complete Bible printed in Scotland.
1590	First paper mill in Scotland established on the Water of Leith.
1603	Union of the crowns. James VI goes to London.
1614	Napier's logarithms printed in Edinburgh.
1622	First printing in Aberdeen, by Edward Raban.
1638	National Covenant. First printing in Glasgow, by George Anderson.
1643	Solemn League and Covenant.
1649	Execution of Charles I.
1651	Charles II crowned king of Scotland. First printing in Leith, by Evan Tyler.
1660/1	*Mercurius Caledonius*, first genuinely Scottish newspaper.
1688	Accession of William and Mary.
1702–14	Reign of Queen Anne.
1707	Union of parliaments.
1710	First copyright act. Advocates' Library in Edinburgh and the four Scottish universities become legal deposit libraries.
1715	Jacobite rising. Robert Freebairn briefly operates a Jacobite press in Perth.
1723	Allan Ramsay, *The Tea-table Miscellany*; three further volumes appeared during the next 14 years.
1739	*Scots Magazine*, Scotland's longest-running magazine, first published in Edinburgh.
1744	Foulis edition of Horace.
1745–46	Jacobite rising under Charles Edward Stuart.
1751	John Smith establishes his bookselling business in Glasgow, which becomes John Smith and Son in 1803.

1757	First printing in Dundee, by Henry Galbraith.
1760	James Macpherson, *Fragments of Ancient Poetry Collected in the Highlands of Scotland, and Translated from the Galic or Erse language* published in Edinburgh.

Macpherson's *Fingal* (1762 edition).

1768	First publication, in Edinburgh, of *Encyclopaedia Britannica*.
1769	James Watt patents his steam engine. Beginning of Industrial Revolution.
1771	Henry Mackenzie, *The Man of Feeling* becomes the most popular British novel of the 1770s.
1772	Printing re-established in Perth, by George Johnston.
1774	First printing in Inverness, by Alexander Davidson.
1783	First publication of *Glasgow Advertiser*, from 1803 *Glasgow Herald*.
1786	Robert Burns's poems printed and published in Kilmarnock.

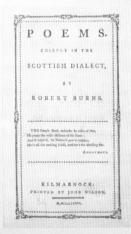

1786

c. 1800–25 Scottish publishers such as Blackwood, Constable, Nelson, Black, Blackie, Chambers, and Collins challenge the domination of London.

1802 *Edinburgh Review* first published. Scott's *Minstrelsy of the Scottish Border* printed in Kelso by James Ballantyne.

1803 First printing in Cupar, Fife, by Robert Tullis, who in 1804 prints for Constable an edition of Fanny Burney, *Evelina*.

1805 Constable publishes Scott's *The Lay of the Last Minstrel*.

1813 Publication of first catalogue of the Hunterian Museum.

1814 Scott's *Waverley* published anonymously. Copyright to last for an author's lifetime plus 28 years.

1817 *Scotsman* and *Blackwood's Edinburgh Magazine* first published. Publication in Glasgow of 'Astronomical Discourses' by Thomas Chalmers, founder in 1843 of the Free Church of Scotland.

1822 George IV's visit to Edinburgh, organised by Scott, effectively establishes the Scottish tartan tradition.

1826 Financial ruin of Ballantyne and Constable, and bankruptcy of Scott.

1827 Scott publicly acknowledges authorship of the Waverley novels.

1832 Death of Sir Walter Scott. Publication of *Chambers's Edinburgh Journal*, the first successful cheap British weekly magazine.

1837–1901 Reign of Queen Victoria.

1842 Copyright extended to life of the author plus seven years, or 42 years from first publication.

1848 James Thin establishes his first bookshop in Edinburgh.

1850 Public Libraries Act.

1854 Public Libraries (Scotland) Act.

1858 R. M. Ballantyne, *The Coral Island* published for young readers.

1860–68 First publication of *Chambers's Encyclopaedia*.

1868 Queen Victoria, *Leaves from the Journal of our Life in the Highlands* boosts the Scottish tourist industry.

1869 First publication in Dundee of the *People's Friend*.

1872 Education Act, Scotland.

1879 R. L. Stevenson, *Travels with a Donkey in the Cévennes* printed in Scotland by Clark.

1911 Copyright extended to life of author plus 50 years.

1915 Ian Hay (John Hay Beith), *The First Hundred Thousand* reflects the spirit of the troops in World War I.

1925 National Library of Scotland established by act of parliament.

1926 Hugh MacDiarmid, *A Drunk Man Looks at the Thistle*.

1929 Neil M. Gunn, *Hidden Doors* published in Edinburgh by Porpoise Press.

1931 Volume One, *The Scottish National Dictionary*, edited by William Grant; Volume Ten was published in 1976.

1935 William Soutar, *Poems in Scots*.

1943 Sorley MacLean (Somhairle MacGill-Eain), *Dàin do Eimhir*.

1948 First publications of Edinburgh University Press.

1954 George Mackay Brown, *The Storm, and Other Poems*, his first book of verse, printed and published in Kirkwall.

1955 Universal Copyright Convention.

1961 Ian Hamilton Finlay, concrete and conceptual poet, founds Wild Hawthorn Press.

1968 Edwin Morgan, *The Second Life: selected poems* contains examples of his concrete poetry.

1981 Alasdair Gray introduces new narrative techniques in *Lanark*, designed and illustrated by himself.

1983 First Edinburgh International Book Festival.

1988 Copyright, Designs and Patents Act. Copyright extended to life plus 70 years.

1996 The film script (by John Hodge) of Irvine Welsh, *Trainspotting* is nominated for an Oscar.

1998 Alexander McCall Smith, *The No. 1 Ladies Detective Agency*.

2004 Edinburgh, first UNESCO City of Literature

THE PEOPLE'S FRIEND

1869

Index

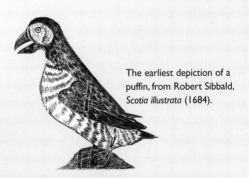

The earliest depiction of a puffin, from Robert Sibbald, *Scotia illustrata* (1684).